Mönche tragen Sandalen.

Monks Wear Sandals.

Christian Heiss

Mönche tragen Sandalen.
Gedanken eines Architekten

Monks Wear Sandals.
Insights of an Architect

Verlag für moderne Kunst

Für meine Frau Shenja – und in sieben Jahren zeichnender Vorfreude auf unsere Tochter Micòl

For Shenja – seven years of drawing spent in anticipation of the joy called Micòl

Erschienen im / Published by
Verlag für moderne Kunst, © 2022
www.vfmk.org
ISBN 978-3-903439-81-8

Von Raum und Zeit

Wir Architekten beobachten gerne, denn unser Beruf umgreift alle Lebensbereiche. Ein Gebäude muss ästhetischen und funktionalen Herausforderungen standhalten und Antworten auf soziale, ökologische und wirtschaftliche Fragen finden.

Die beste Methode, Gedanken freien Lauf zu lassen und Ideen für einen Entwurf zu entwickeln, ist das Skizzieren. Unsere Sprache sind also schwarze Linien auf weißem Papier. Daraus können schließlich Pläne entstehen, nach denen gebaut wird.

Of Space and Time

We architects love to observe – after all, our profession has a bearing on all areas of life. A building has to meet aesthetic and functional challenges and provide answers to social, ecological, and economic questions.

The most effective method to give free rein to one's thoughts and to develop ideas for a draft is sketching. Our language therefore boils down to black lines on white paper. These may develop into blueprints that are realised.

When ideas take shape in the form of lines and, ultimately, in the form

Wenn Gedanken sich zu Linien und schließlich zu Raum formen, bereichert durch Sonnenlicht, Akustik und viele andere Zutaten, begeistert mich das immer wieder aufs Neue. Aus einer Idee entsteht Leben.

Meine Zeichnungen in diesem Buch sind zu Papier gebrachte Gedanken, Stimmungen, Fragen. Da die meisten von ihnen durchaus mehrdeutig sind, habe ich sie von Anfang an Cartoons genannt, auch weil sie zum Schmunzeln anregen sollen.

Ein Cartoon ist schnell gezeichnet. Es gibt keine Recherche, kein

of space, enriched by sunlight, acoustics, and many other ingredients, this still makes my head spin with enthusiasm. An idea morphs into a living organism.

My drawings in this book are ideas, moods, questions jotted down on paper. As most of them are packed with more than one meaning, I have always referred to them as cartoons. They are designed to make you smile.

A cartoon is completed in no time at all. There is no research, no preliminary drawing, no auxiliary lines, no revision. Of each cartoon there is only one version. Some days see the birth of

Vorzeichnen, keine Hilfslinien, kein Korrigieren. Jedes Blatt wird nur einmal gezeichnet. Manchmal gelingen mehrere am Tag, manchmal nur eins oder zwei im Monat. Viele sind auf Reisen entstanden. Sieben Jahre und 1000 Cartoons: für mich eine Art sehr persönliches Tagebuch – und zudem sind nun alle Fragen des Lebens endlich beantwortet ...

several cartoons, sometimes it's only one or two in a whole month. Many of them have come into being during travels. Seven years and 1000 cartoons: a highly personal diary – and, believe it or not, the definitive answer to all of life's most pressing questions ...

Christian Heiss

083 und das Geheimnis von Stift und Papier

Christian Heiss ist ein großer Mann (105), ein richtiger Giacometti (138), keinesfalls kugelrund, denn dazu tut er viel zu viel (270), sondern so richtig mit begnadetem Körper (272) und François-Gesicht (166, 236) – mit Lächeln (109), Barthaaren (033, 079) und dem Schalk im Auge (164). Kennengelernt haben wir uns vor tausend Jahren, vor einer wirklich langen Zeit (042), als wir uns erstmals über Pommes (311), Kraftsuppen (080) und McSundae-Sahneberge (171) unterhalten haben. Am Anfang war das Wort (024), und schon damals – er noch ein ganzes Kind (202),

083 and a Secret Shared Between Pen and Paper

Christian Heiss is tall (105), a proper Giacometti (138). Not round as a barrel (270) – he is much too active for that. He has a sublime body (272) and a François face (166, 236) – with a smile (109), whiskers (033, 079), and a roguish twinkle in his eye (164). We first met a really long time ago, like 1000 years ago (042), and we talked about French fries (311), the power of soup (080), and McSundae cream mountains (171). In the beginning was the word (024), and even then I thought – he was still a child (202), a young apple (100), a tender plant (093) in the profession:

ein junger Apfel (100), ein zartes Pflänzchen (093) in der Branche – dachte ich mir: Mit so viel Liebe zum Detail (068), was für ein Zauberer der Räume (230)!

Keine Ahnung, ob er je Ruhe geben kann (055), bewegtes Leben (045), das Hirn immer voll (070), nie in Ermangelung von Ideen (229). Doch nach vielen geplanten und gebauten Schneckenhäusern (035) hat er nun, in einem Moment des Wimpernschlags (095), offenbar beschlossen, seinem Dasein eine zweite Pistazie zu geben (170). Eh schon ein Leben voller Höhepunkte (136), längst oben angekommen (137), aber nein, er muss ausbrechen (153), frei wie ein

With such a love of detail (068) he is handling space like a magician (230)!

No idea whether he can ever keep quiet (055), molto agitato (045), the brain always full (070), never at a loss for ideas (229). But after all the snail's houses he has designed and built (035), in the blink of an eye (095) he now appears to have decided to give his existence a second pistachio (170). A life full of high points (136) and having made it to the top (137) is not enough, no, he must make a run for it (153), free as a bird (246), in a world of his own (074) and, on top of everything, with such an absurd idea (133) – a diary with moon and stars (301), in a totally

Vogel (246), in eine ganz eigene Welt (074), und dann auch noch so eine absurde Idee (133) – ausgerechnet ein Tagebuch mit Mond und Sternen (301), in einer ganz anderen Sprache als bisher (189). Die Gier ist ein Hund (063).

Aber, Respekt (182), lieber Christian, du bist eine eierlegende Wollmilch-sau (226)! Und wenn du so die Seele baumeln lässt (046) und deine Lebensgeister (135) das Geheimnis von Stift und Papier entdecken (083), dann kann man einfach nicht wegschauen (210). Alles, was du fest-halten willst (044) in diesem offenen Buch (101), in all deinen leichten Welt-bildern (114), ob groß oder klein (059),

unfamiliar language (189) compared to anything that has gone before. Greed is a savage beast (063).

But respect where respect is due (182), dear Christian, you are that egg-laying, lactating woolly sow (226)! And when you allow your soul to dangle (046) and when your spirits of life (135) discover the secret of pen and paper (083), looking away is not an option (210). The things you want to save for a rainy day (044) in this open book (101), in all your light world views (114), big or small (059), are simple (071) and at the same time deeply touching (090, 132, 177), even though some may give the impression

auch wenn manche davon unvollendet wirken (032), ist einfach (071) und doch berührend (090, 132, 177). Wenige Striche sind genug (050).

Jetzt hast auch du den Schweinehund besiegt (084) und selbst ein Buch geschrieben (118)! Ein schönes Lebenswerk (207), mögest du diesen Schatz weitergeben (205)!

of being unfinished (032). A little is plenty (050).

You have now bested your weaker self (084) by writing a book yourself (118)! A wonderful life's work (207)! May you pass on this treasure (205)!

Wojciech Czaja (116)

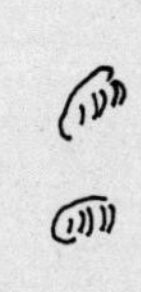

Monks wear sandals.

MÖNCHE TRAGEN SANDALEN.

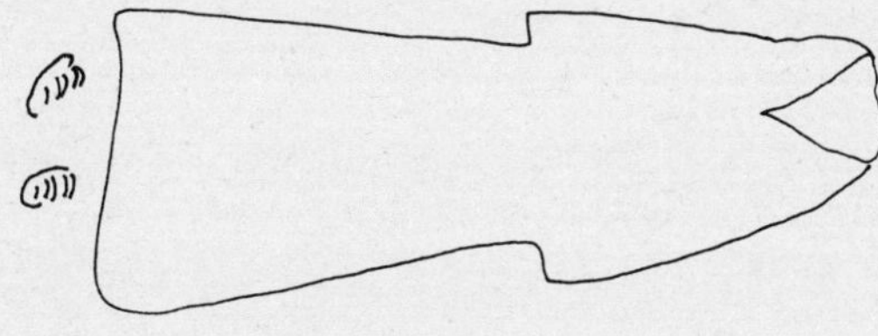

AUCH
STARS
HABEN
ORANGEN-
HAUT.

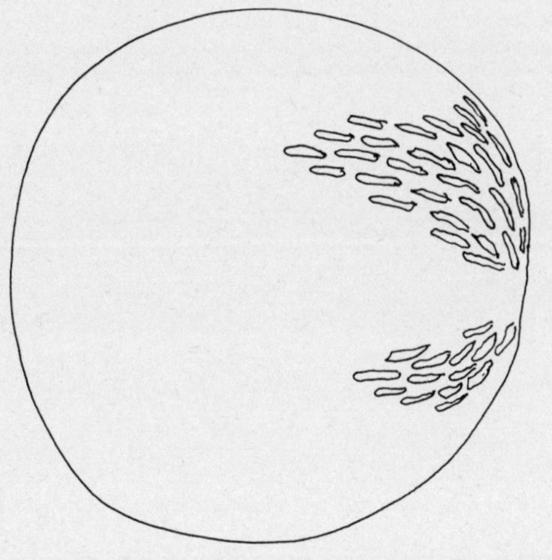

Stars are just as susceptible to orange skin.

Climb all eight-thousanders? Why?

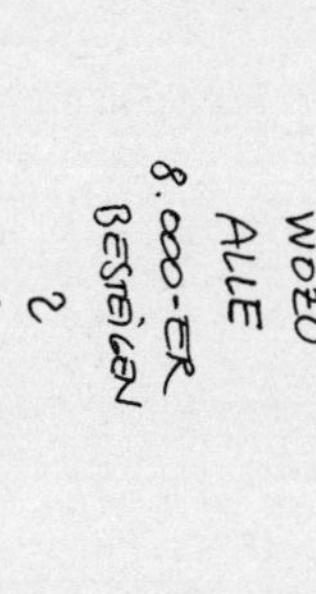

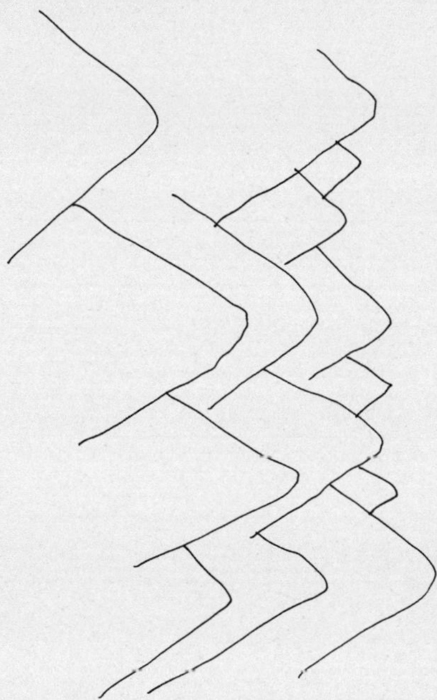

GESPENSTER
SIEHT
MAN
NICHT.

Ghosts are invisible.

023

Every heart looks different.

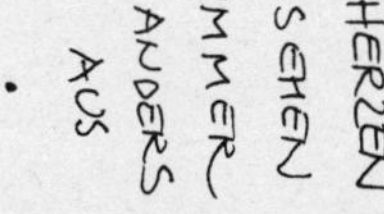

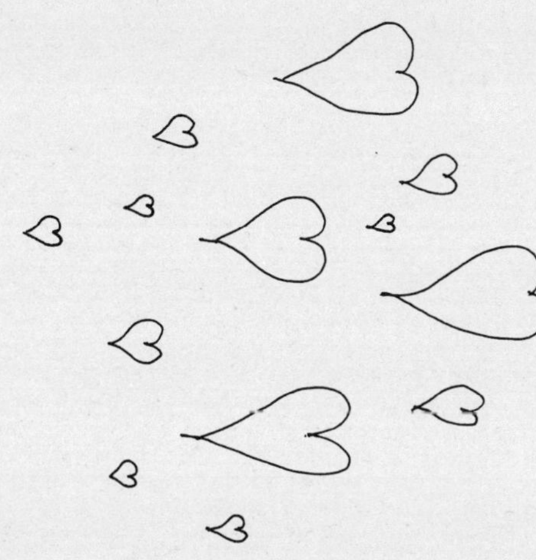

AM
ANFANG
IST
DAS
WORT
.

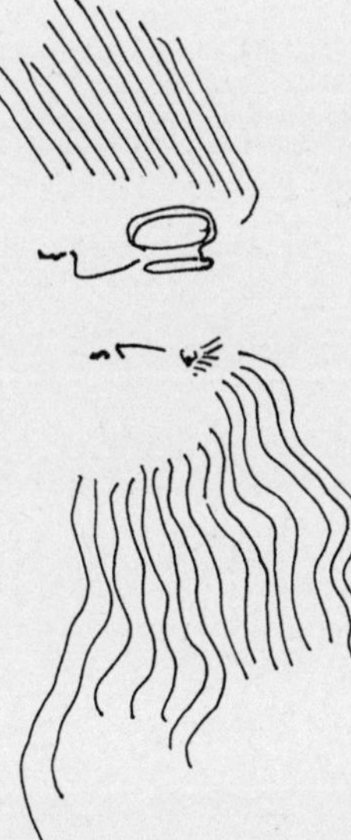

In the beginning was the word.

Let the tears fall.

TRÄNEN
SOLLEN
TROPFEN.

SIND
BÄUME
ABENDS
MÜDE
?

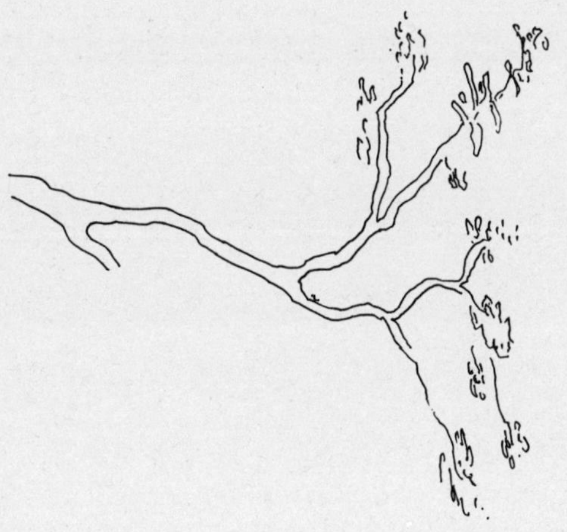

Are trees tired in the evening?

The genie from the glass.

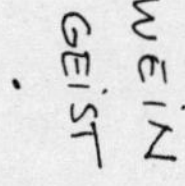

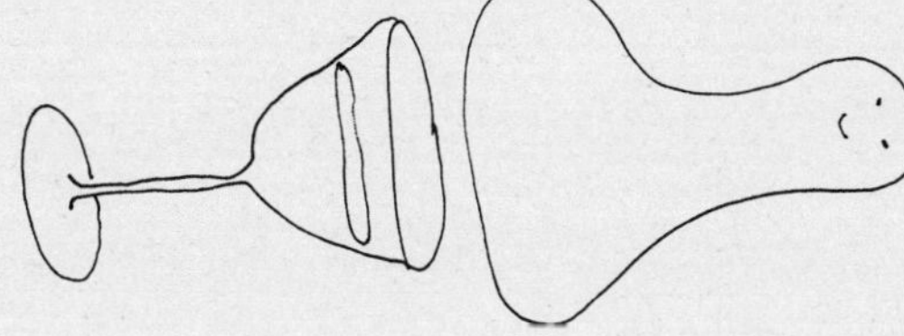

LEITUNGS-
WASSER:
WUNDER
DER
STADT.

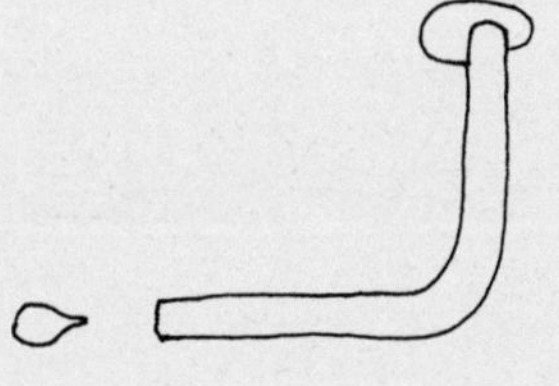

Tap water: urban marvel.

Honour is an ancient word.

Ehre

IST
EIN
ALTES
WORT
.

FREUNDSCHAFT
IST
DER
SEGEN
DER
STERNE
.

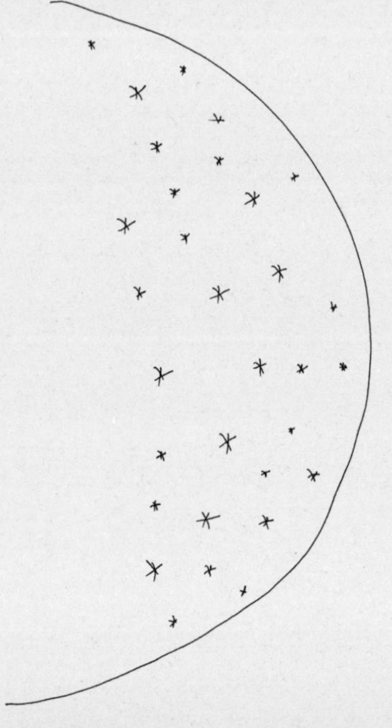

Friendship is the blessing of the stars.

Bald heads are smooth.

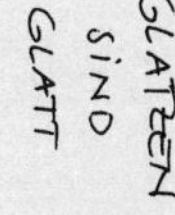

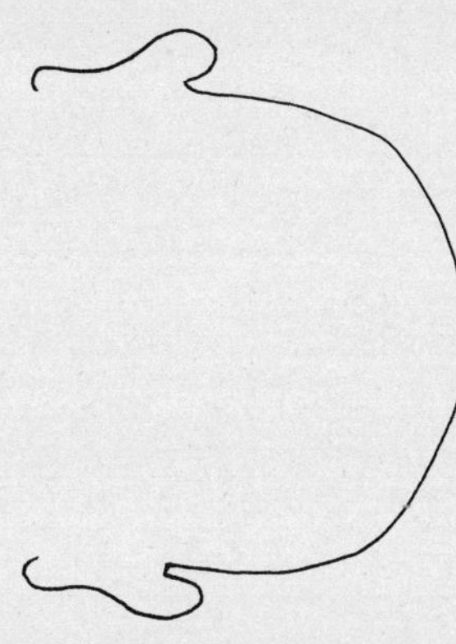

UN
VOLL
ENDET.

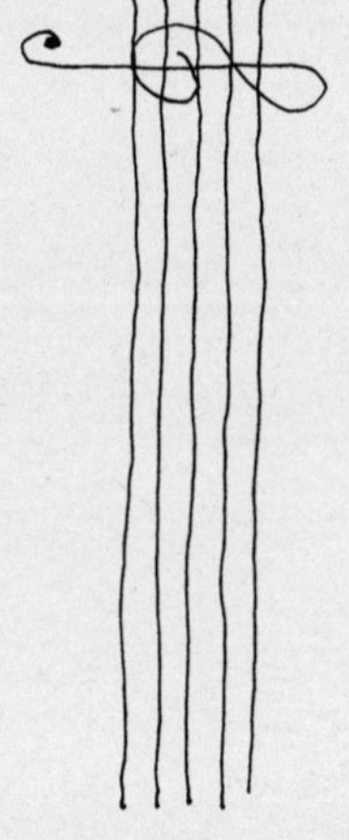

Unfinished.

033

Shaving kills the beard.

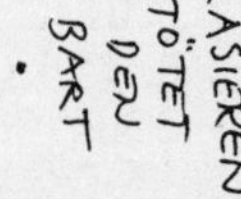

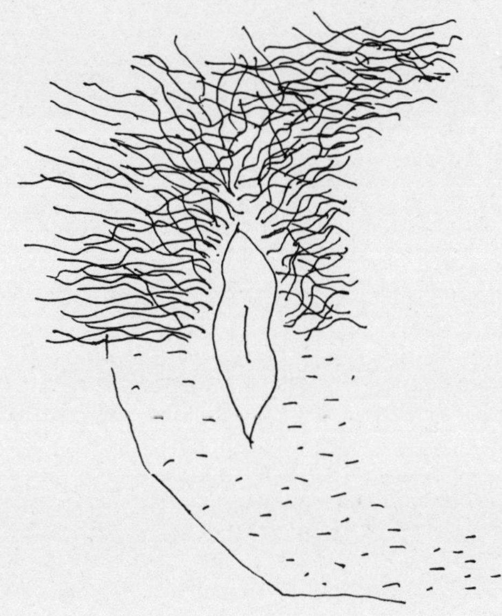

FLEISCH
KONNTE
VORHER
LAUFEN
.

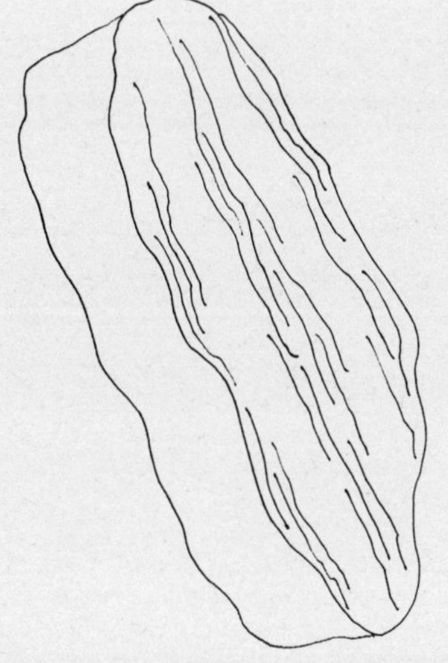

Time was when meat could run.

035 Snails love their houses.

SCHNECKEN
LIEBEN
IHRE
HÄUSER
.

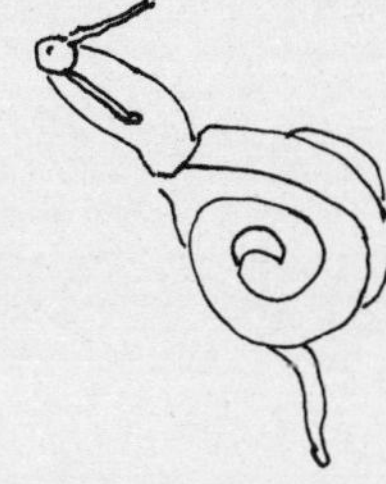

SCHLAFEN
ERMÖGLICHT
TRÄUME.

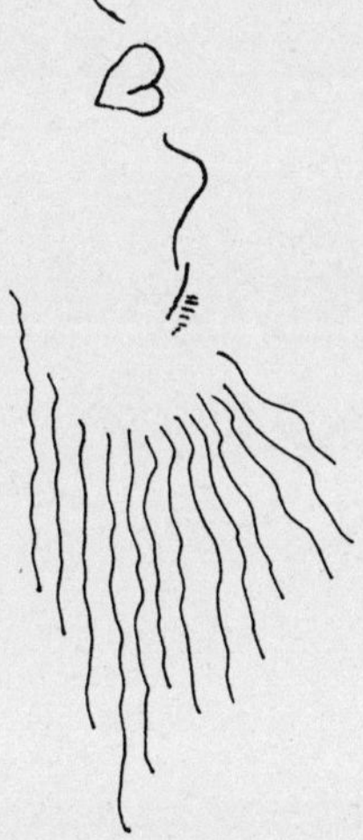

To sleep, perchance to dream.

037

Ants are streets, too.

AMEISEN
SIND
AUCH
STRASSEN
.

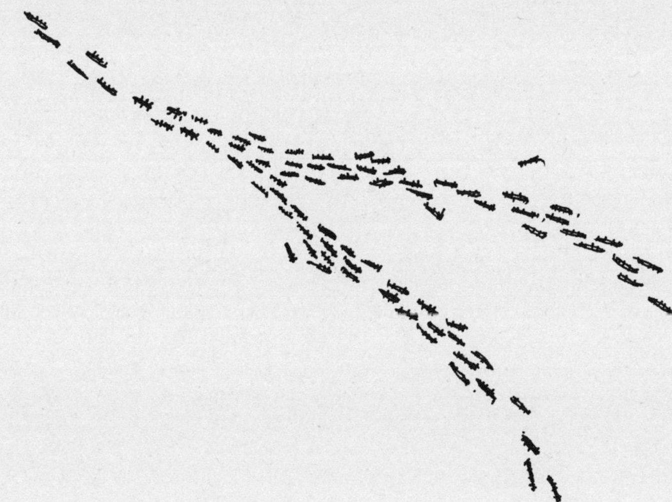

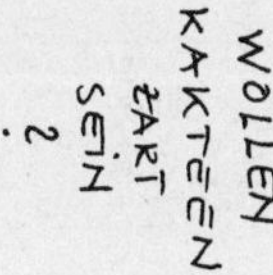

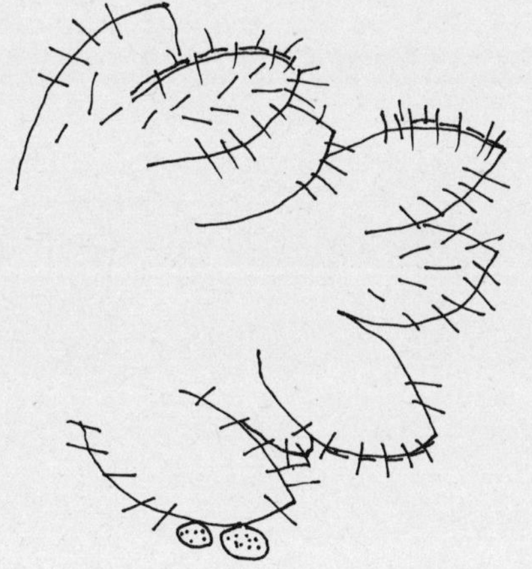

Do cacti dream of being tender?

Are there fat elephants?

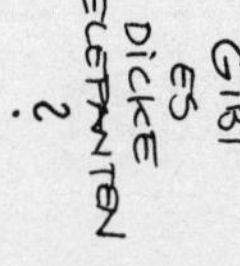

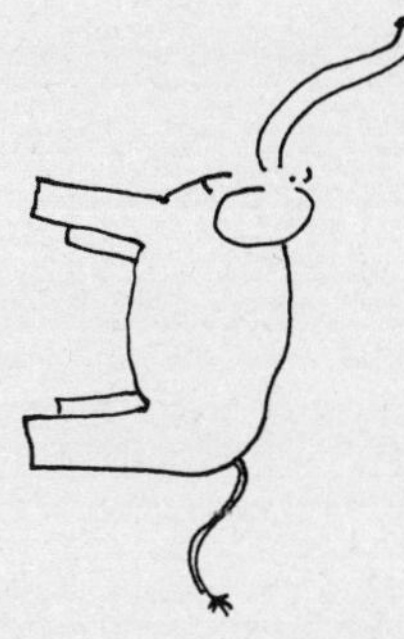

FISCHE
WISSEN,
WIE
GROSS
IHR
MEER
IST.

Fish know how big their ocean is.

SEELE
SCHMÜCKT
SCHMUCK.

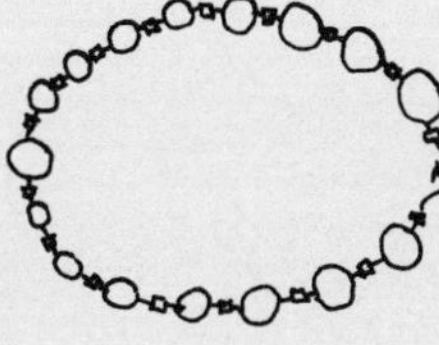

1000
JAHRE
SIND
EINE
SEHR
LANGE
ZEIT
.

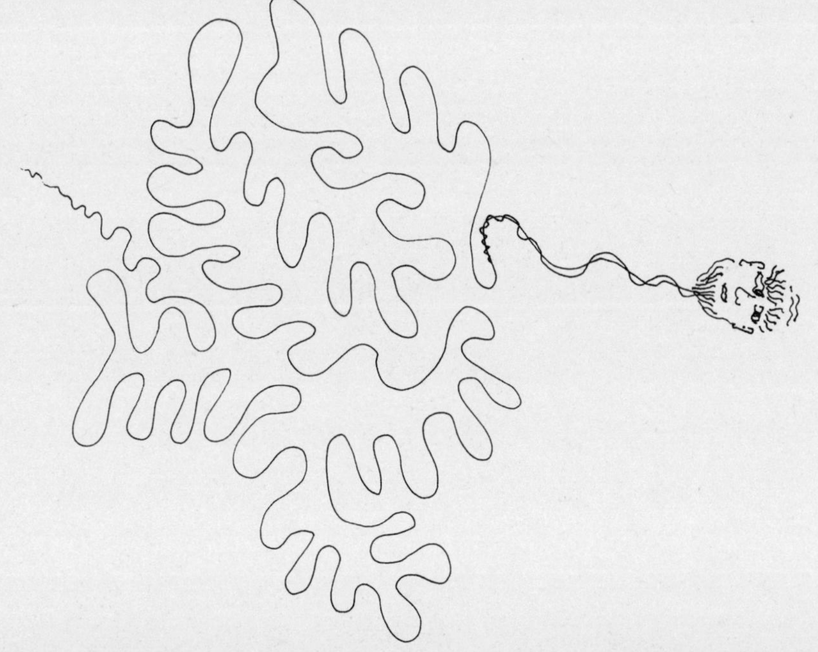

1000 years is a long time indeed.

1000 years is not that long.

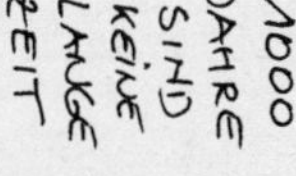

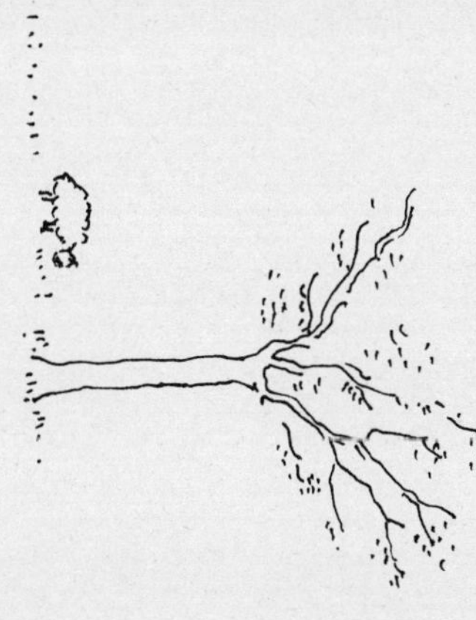

FEST
HALTEN
WOLLEN.

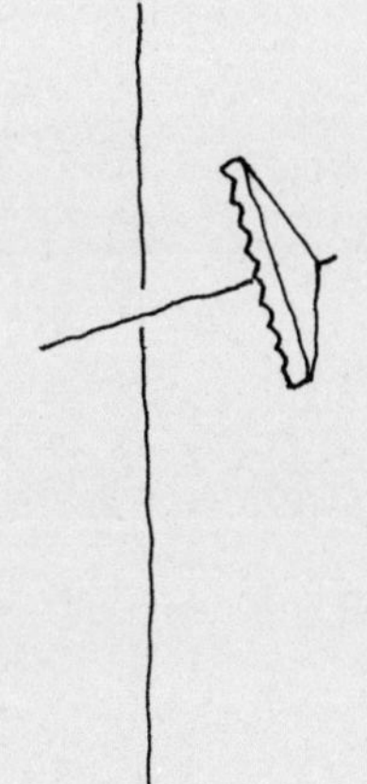

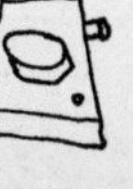

Saving it for a rainy day.

045

Molto agitato.

BEWEGTES
LEBEN.

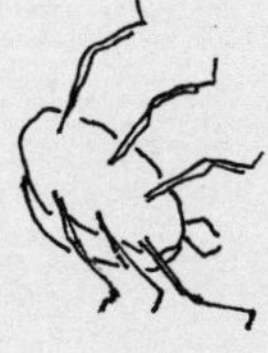

ALLE
SEELEN
MÜSSEN
BAUMELN.

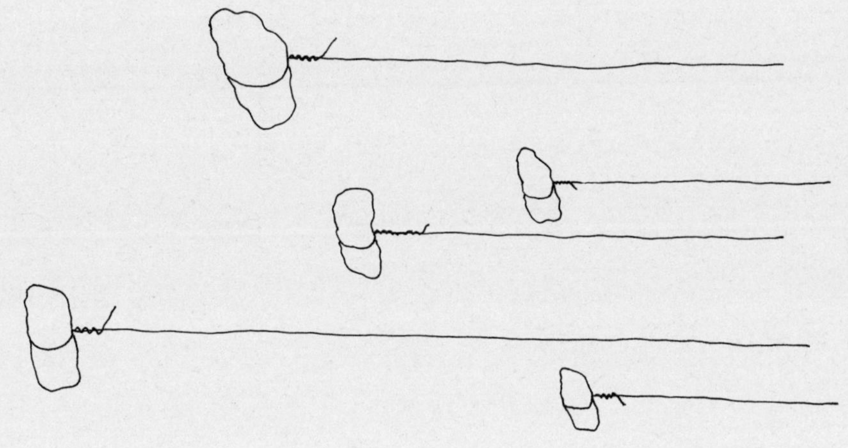

All souls need to dangle.

047 Even in the lazy, there's a beating heart. Always.

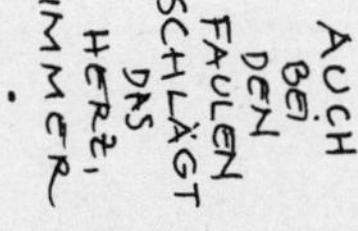

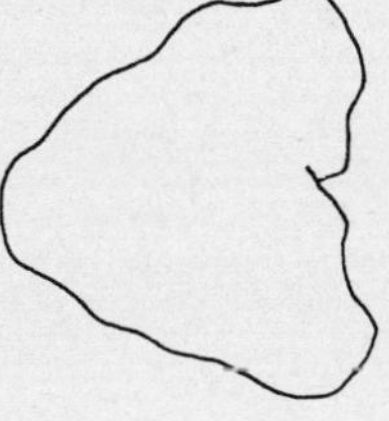

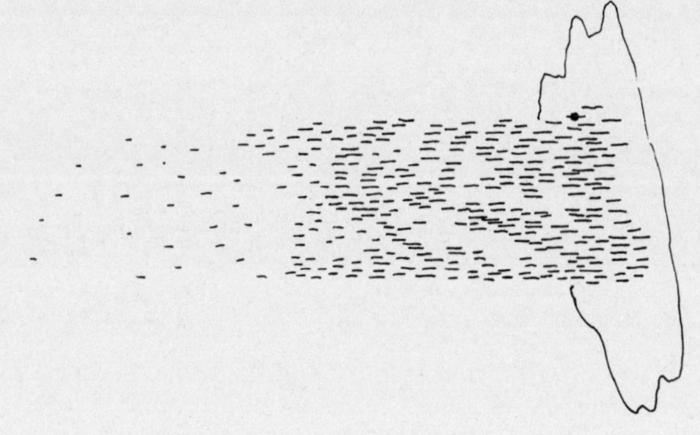

REGNET'S
IMMER
IRGEDWO
?

Is it always raining somewhere?

In reality, the sun never sets.

IN
WIRKLICHKEIT
GEHT
DIE
SONNE
NIE
UNTER
.

WENIG
IST
GENUG.

A little is plenty.

Music is everywhere.

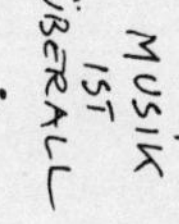

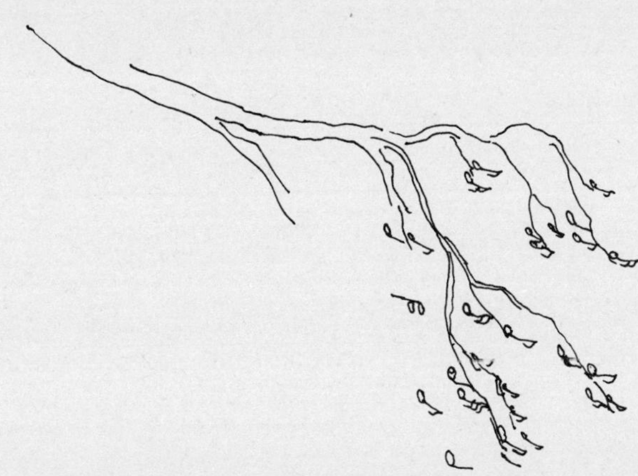

AUCH
JOBS
WERDEN
KEINE
100.

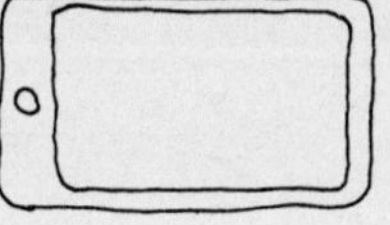

Jobs don’t get to live to a hundred, either.

A life.

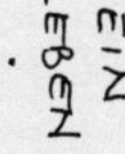

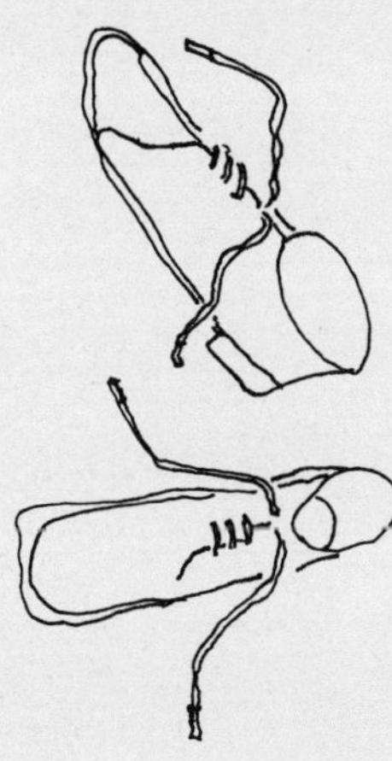

WOZU
IM
LOTTO
GEWINNEN
WOLLEN
?

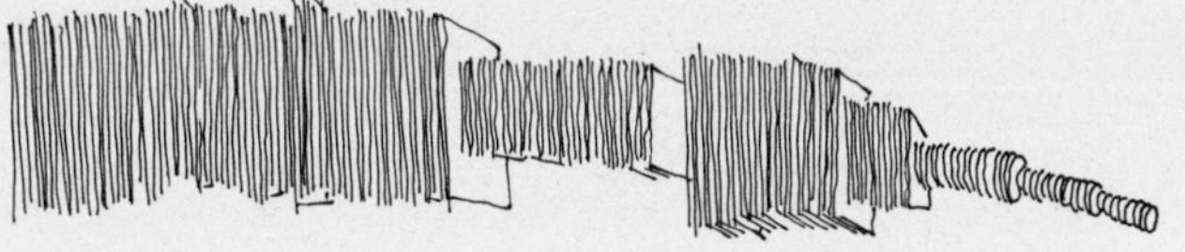

Why would you want to win the lottery?

Quiet.

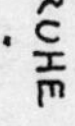

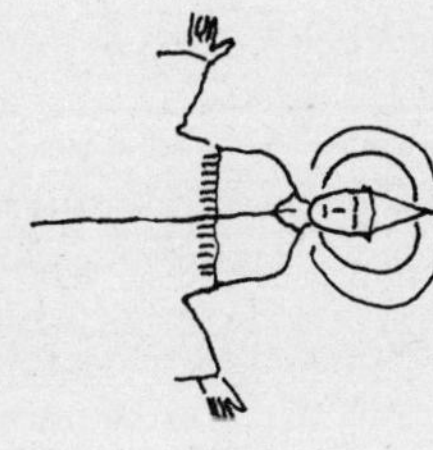

SPAREN
KANN
MAN
ÜBERALL

There's nothing you can't economise on.

057 Life weighs you down.

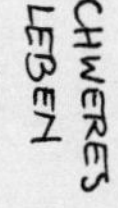

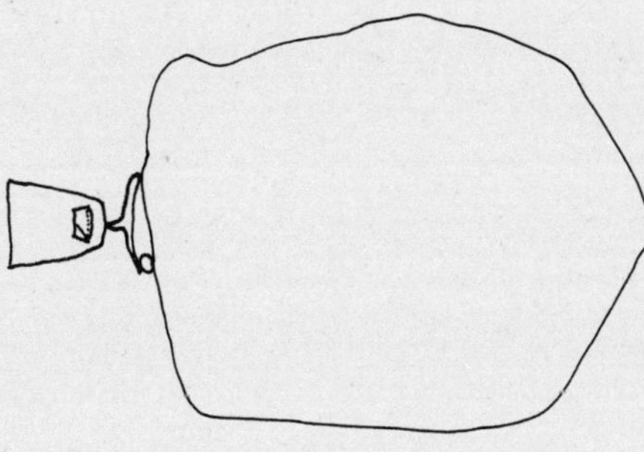

LEICHTES
LEBEN.

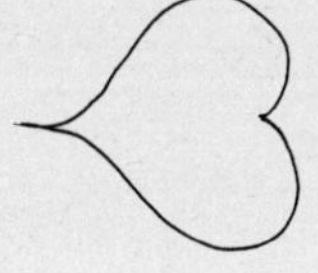

Life buoys you up.

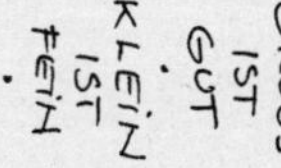
GROSS
IST
GUT
.
KLEIN
IST
FEIN
.

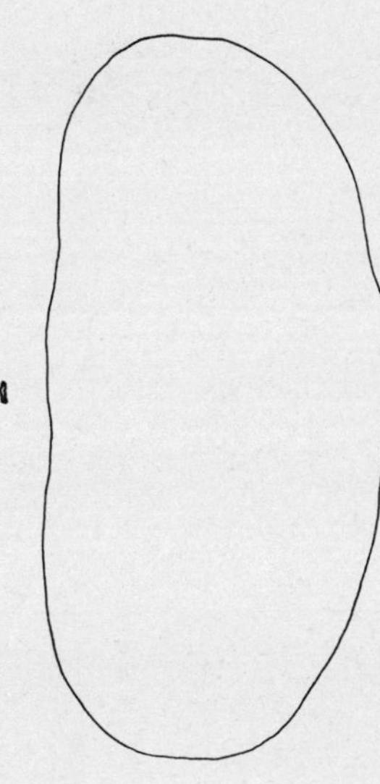

SEI'S
WIE'S
SEI,
STIRBT
KUH
BLEIBT'S
HEI.

(KÄRNTNER WEISHEIT)
HEI = HEU

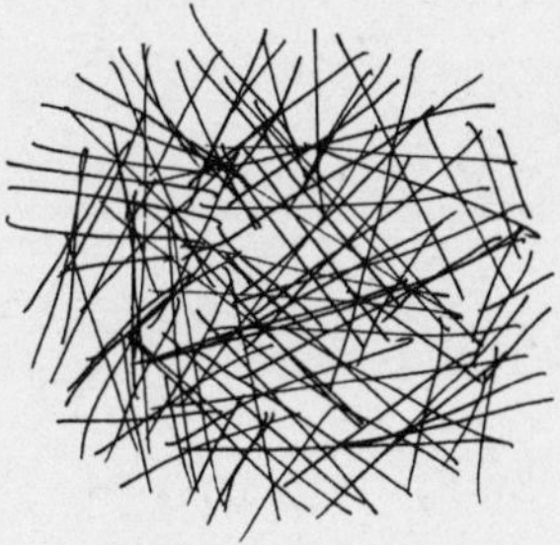

 Be that as it may, if the cow dies, you've still got the hay. (Saying from Carinthia)

061 There’s no way you can delegate sleeping.

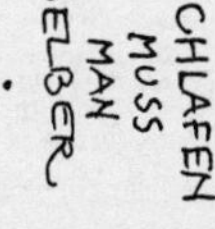

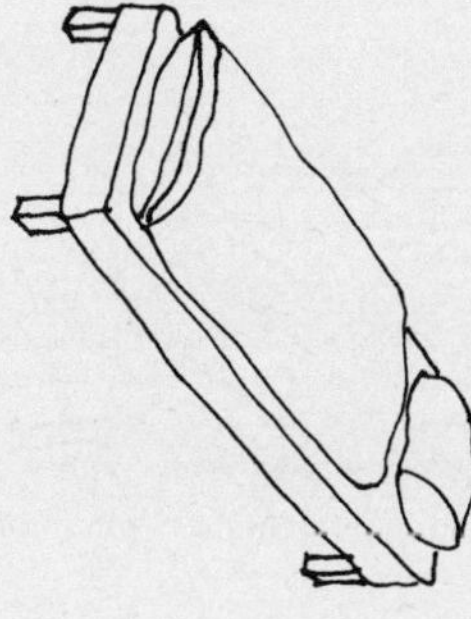

MAN
KANN
KEINE
40
TASSEN
KAFFEE
TRINKEN,
LEIDER.

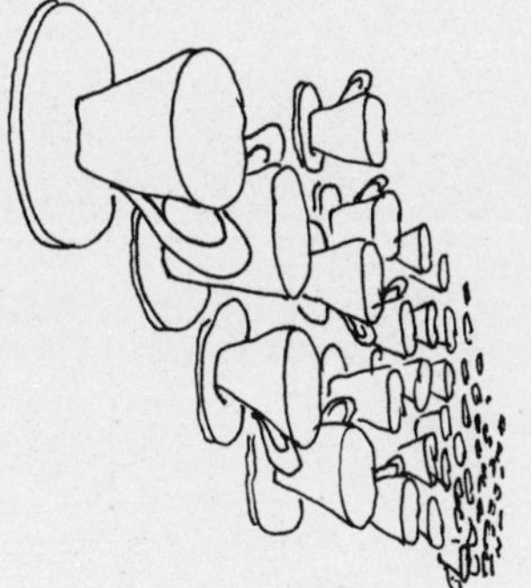

There's no way you can drink 40 cups of coffee. Pity!

063

Greed is a savage beast.

DIE
GIER
IST
EIN
HUND.

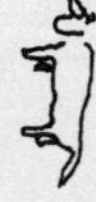

FAST ALLES HAT EINEN PREIS.

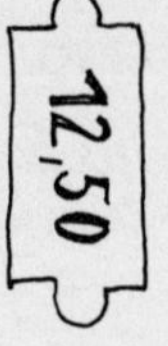

Almost everything has a price.

Father Christmas has no birthday.

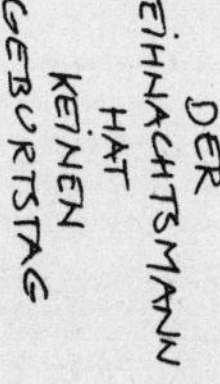

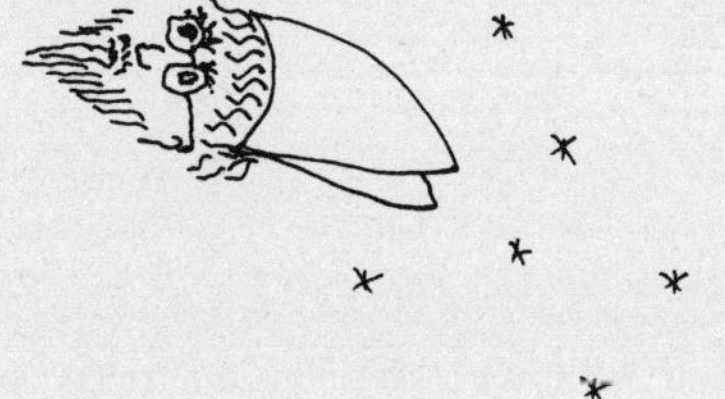

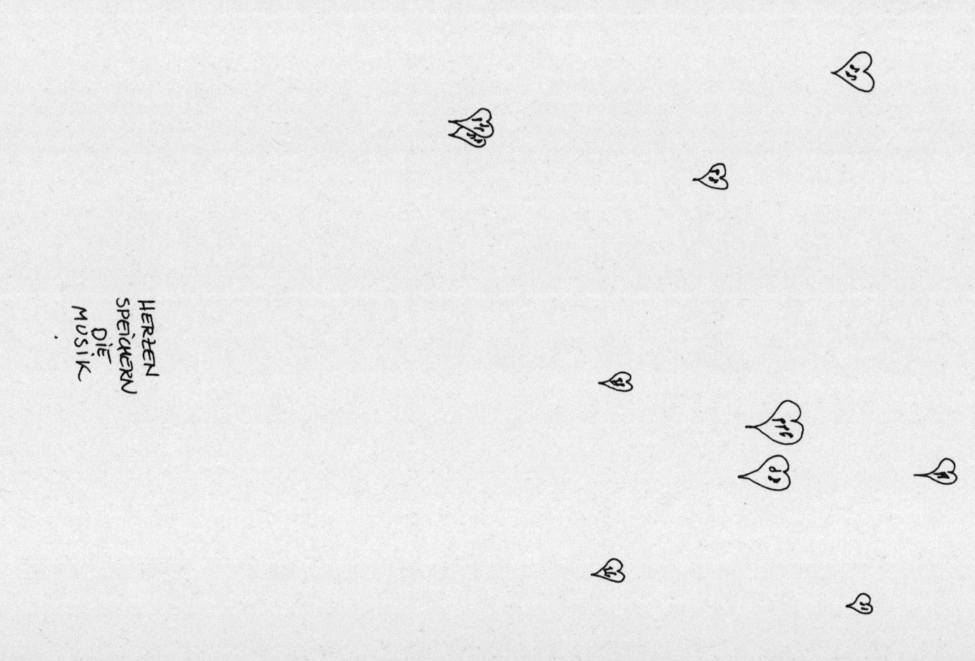

Hearts store the music.

Hearts on the lookout.

HERZEN SEHEN.

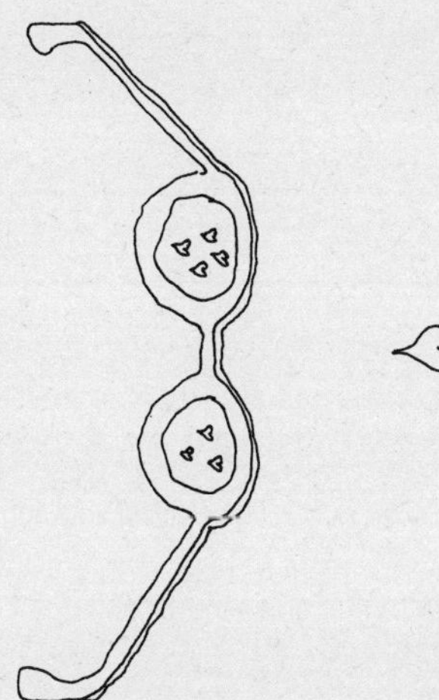

LIEBE
ZUM
DETAIL.

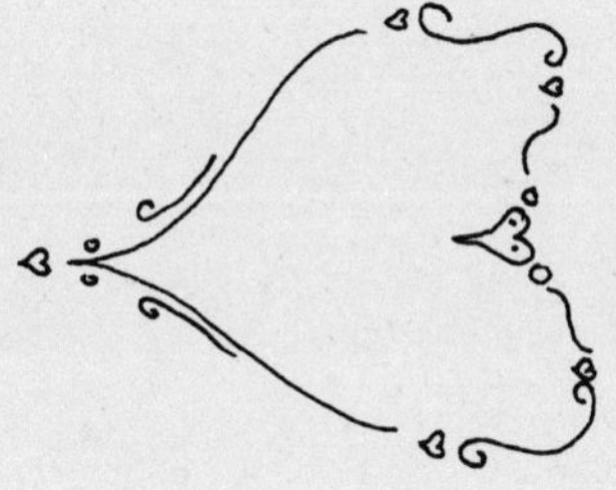

068 Love of detail.

Silicone breasts on stand-by.

SILIKONBRÜSTE
ALS
ZWEITES
STANDBEIN.

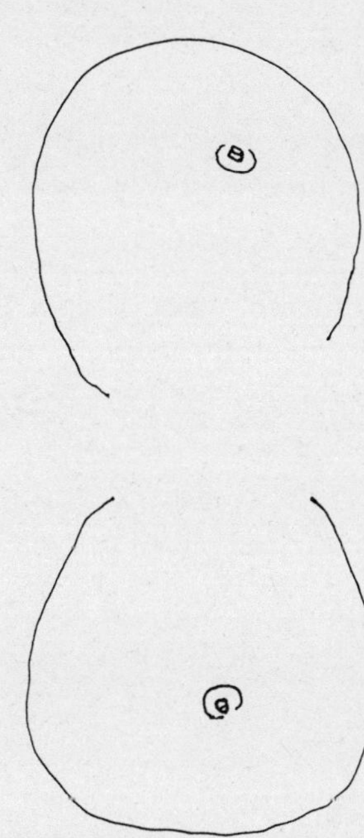

HiRN
VOLL.

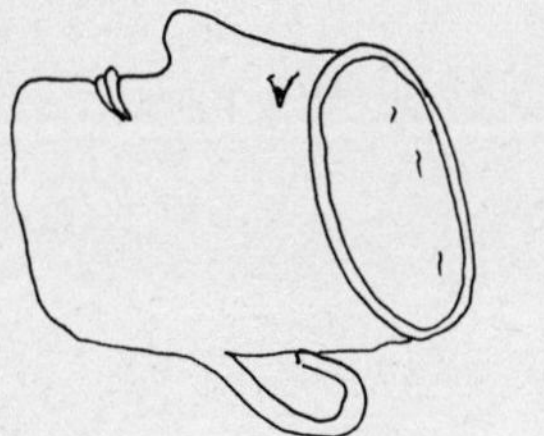

A brainful.

Simple.

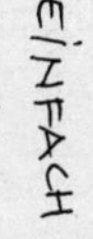

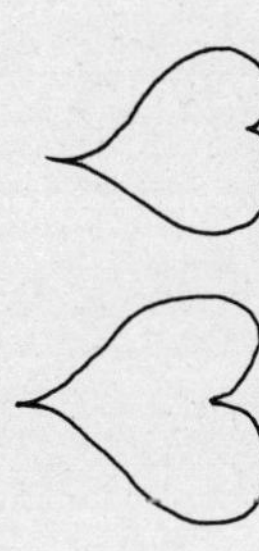

PFLÄNZCHEN
BRAUCHEN
REGEN.

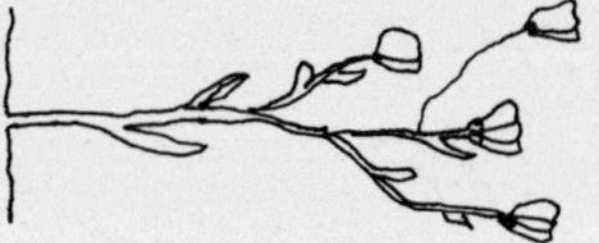

Young plants need rain.

Long neck.

LANGER HALS.

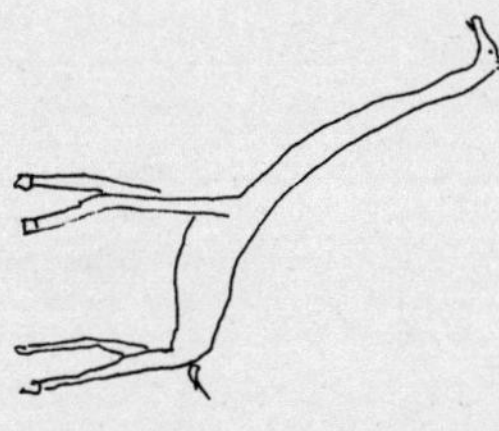

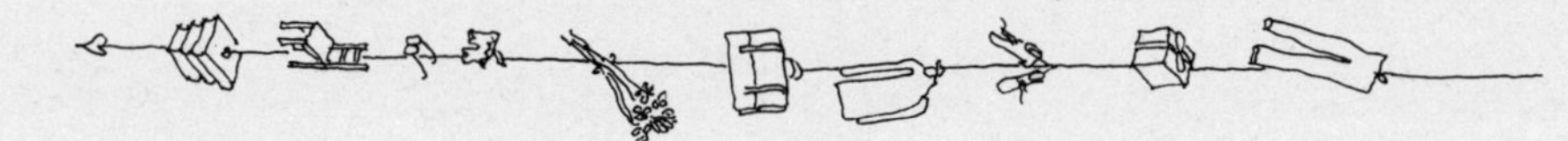

A world of one's own.

Magnifying time.

ZEIT
LUPE

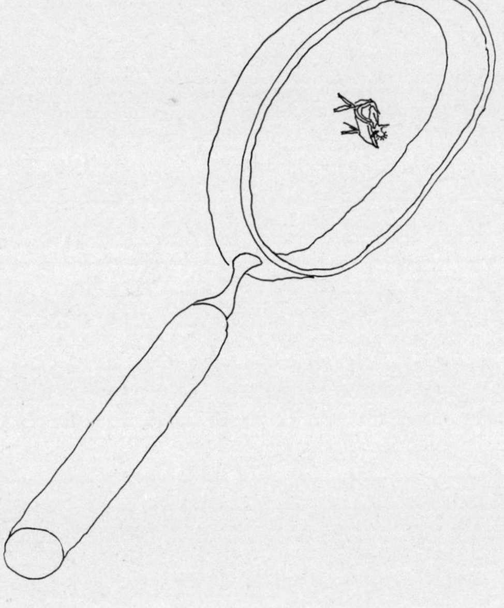

BILDER HABEN.

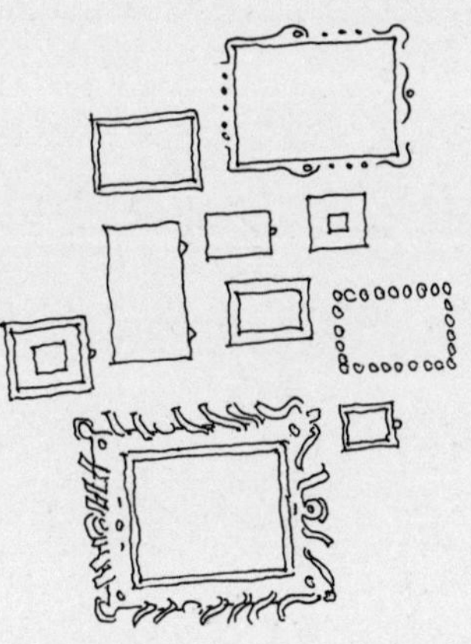

Collecting pictures.

077 Rooted.

VERWURZELT.

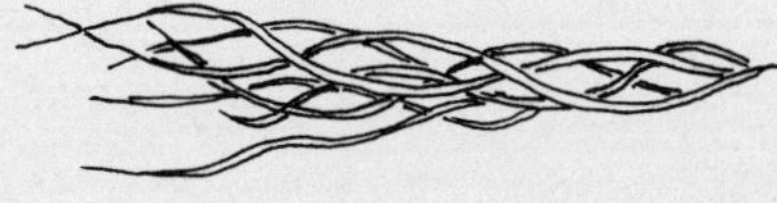

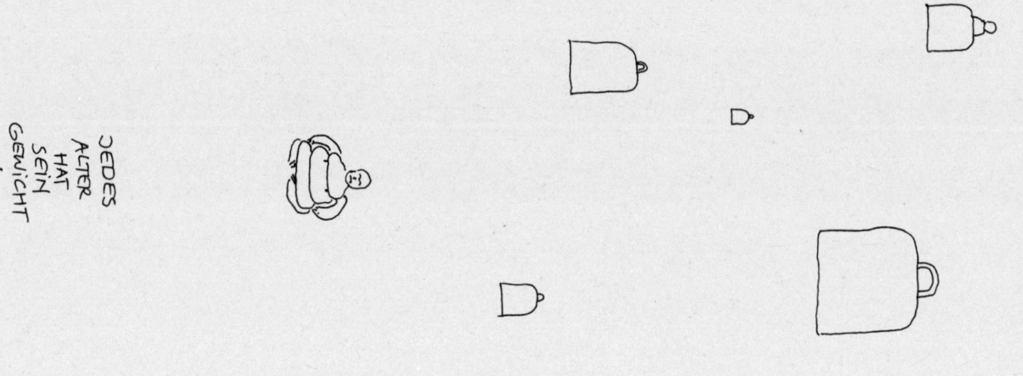

Each age has its own weight.

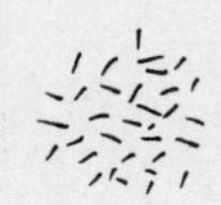

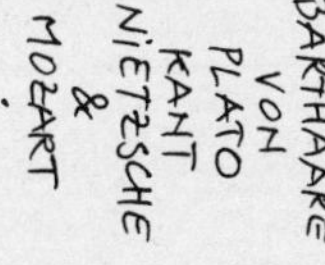
BARTHAARE
VON
PLATO
KANT
NIETZSCHE
&
MOZART.

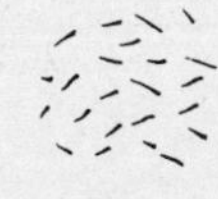

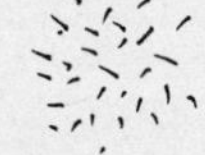

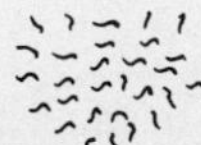

DIE
KRAFT
DER
SUPPE.

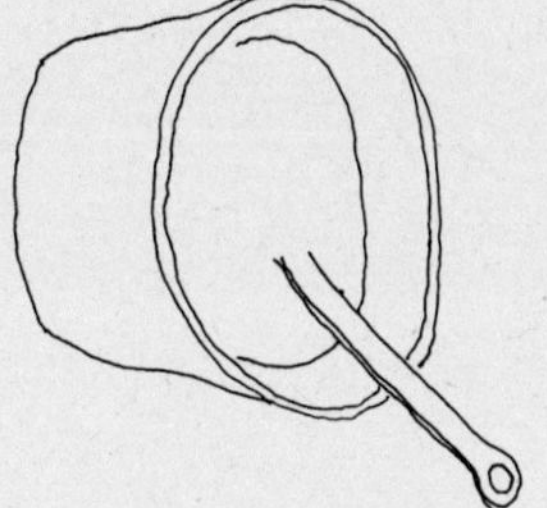

The power of soup.

Clowns are just as sad.

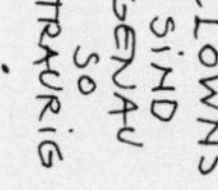

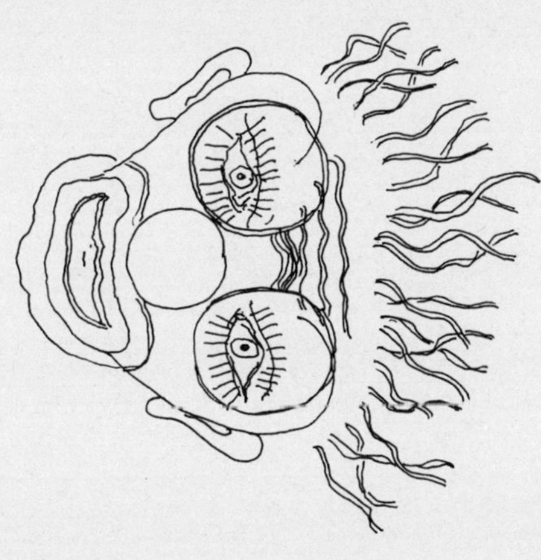

BÄUME IN DER SCHULE.

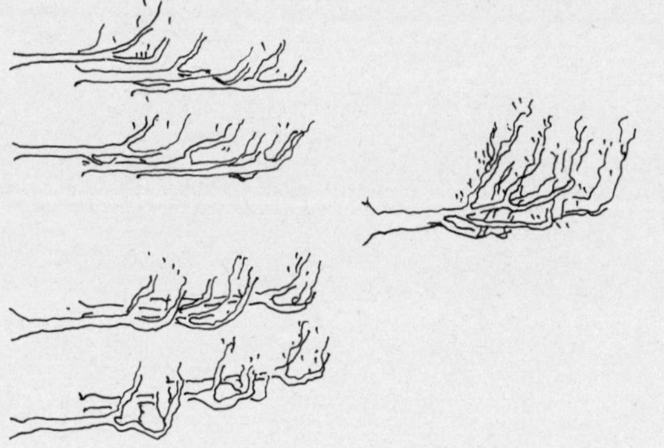

Trees being taught a lesson.

083

A secret shared between pen and paper.

GEHEIMNIS VON STIFT UND PAPIER.

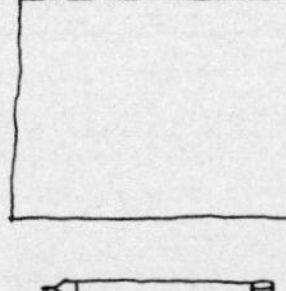

DER
SCHWEINEHUND.

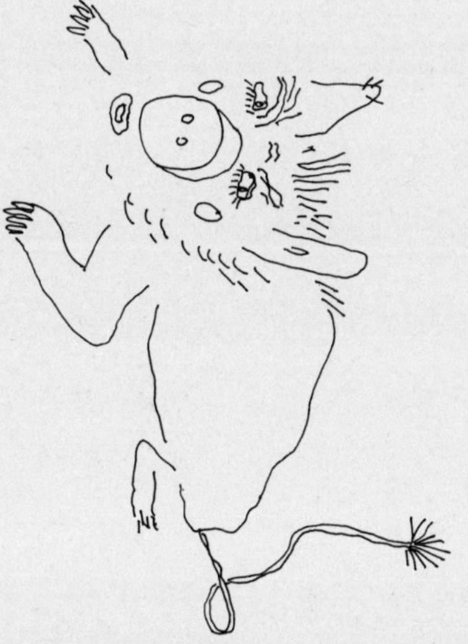

One's weaker self.

Pollen.

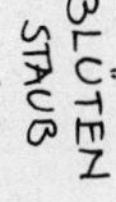

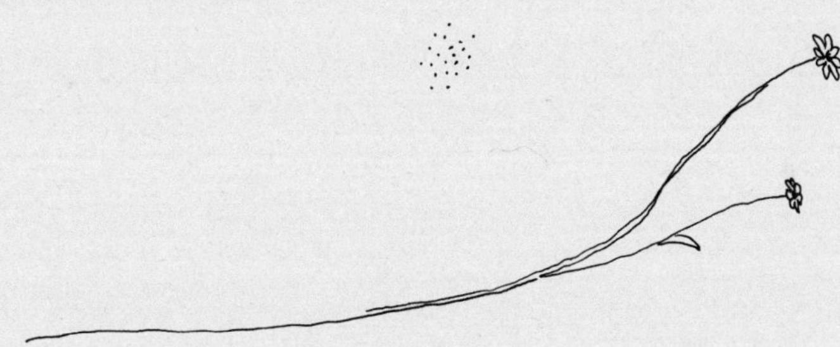

IRGENDWANN GEHT DER DECKEL ZU.

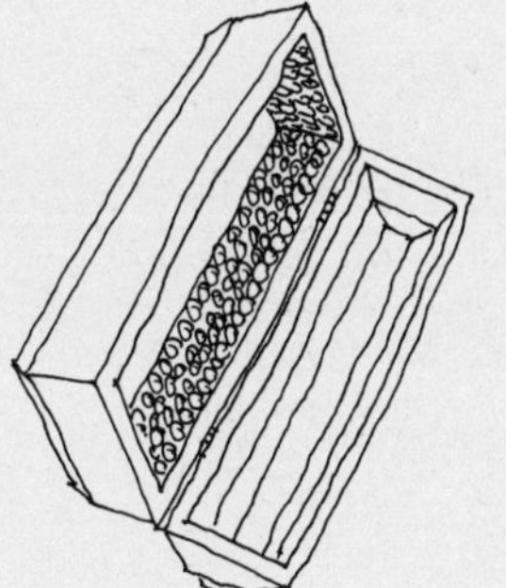

At some stage the lid comes down.

Deer have a lot on their mind.

HIRSCHE
HABEN
VIEL
AM
KOPF
.

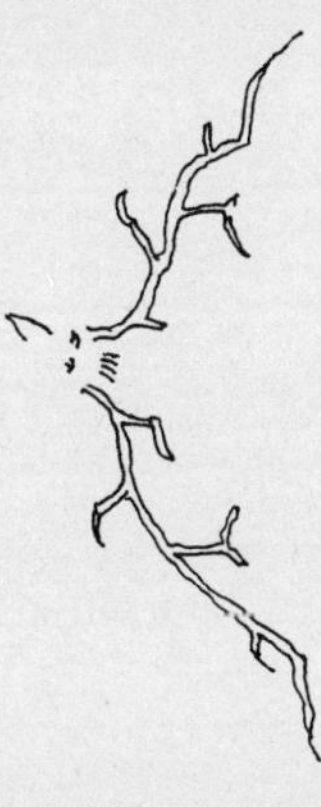

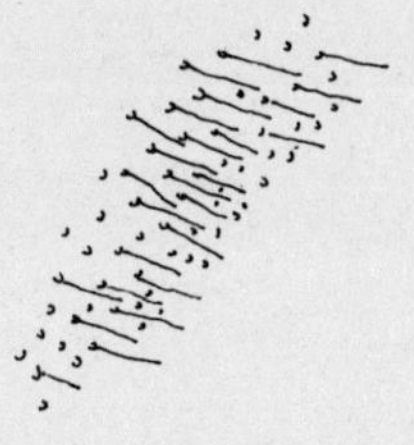

Goosebumps.

All shirts have been chosen.

ALLE
HEMDEN
WURDEN
AUSERWÄHLT.

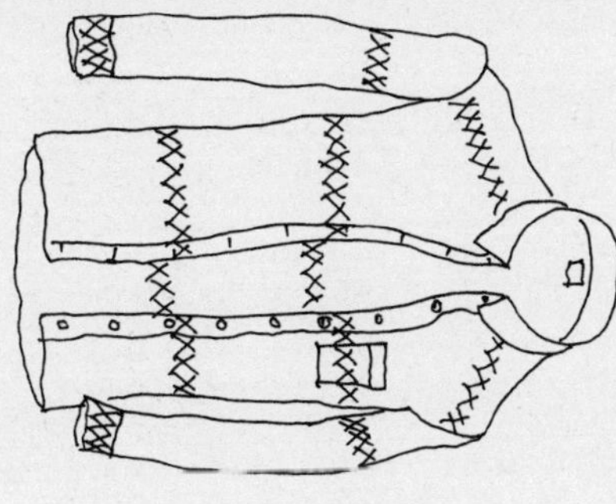

BERÜHREND

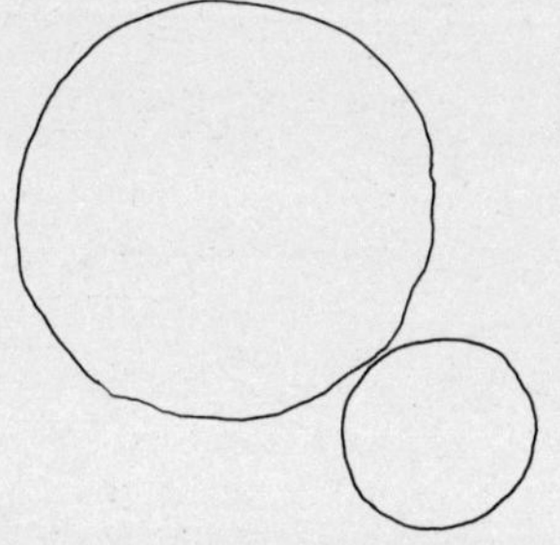

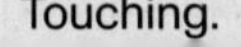

Touching.

Virgil, the old raven, only spoke Latin.

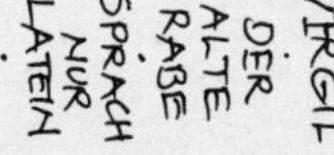

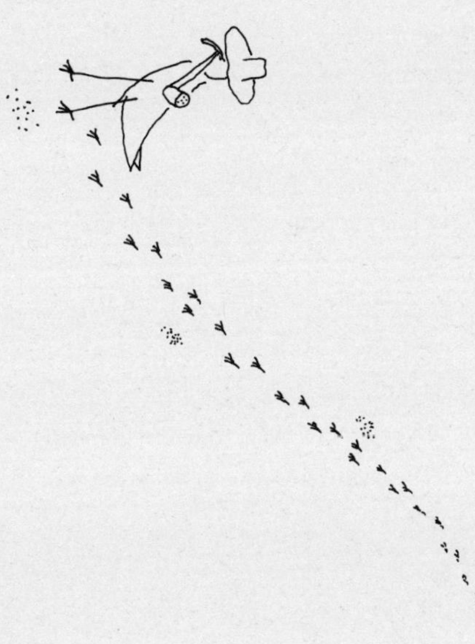

NASE
MIT
HERZ.

092 A nose with a heart.

Tender plants.

ZARTES
PFLÄNZCHEN.

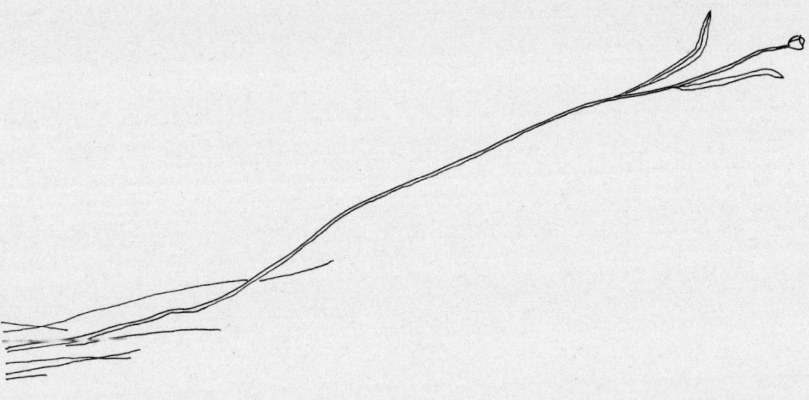

BLÖD
WIE
EIN
STOCK.

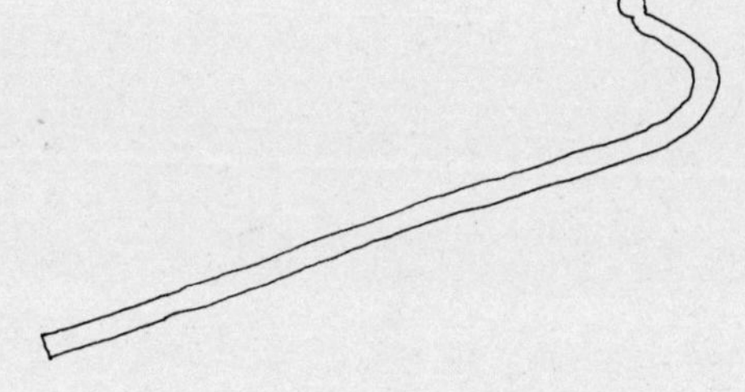

Thick as a stick.

In the blink of an eye.

WIMPERN
SCHLAG.

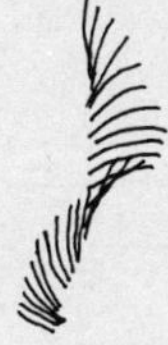

NUDEL
LIEBE.

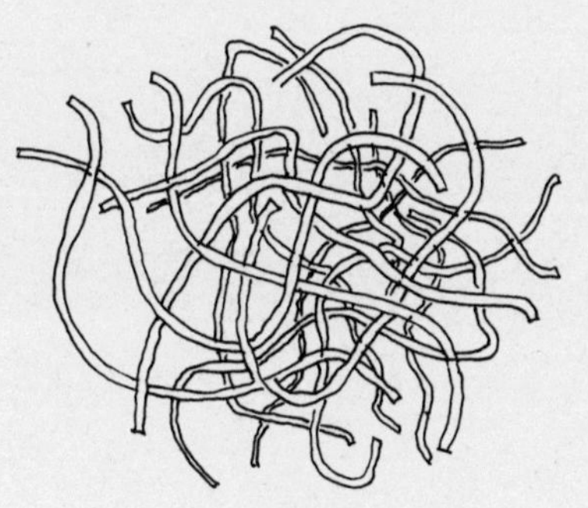

Noodle love.

Plant love.

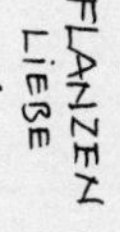

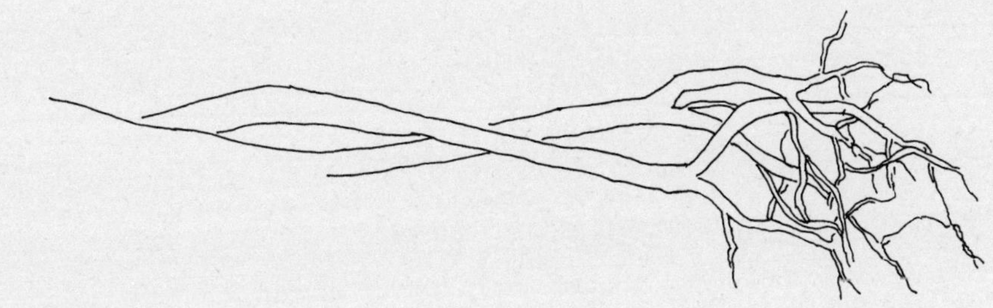

ENDLICH:
OVALE
TOMATEN.

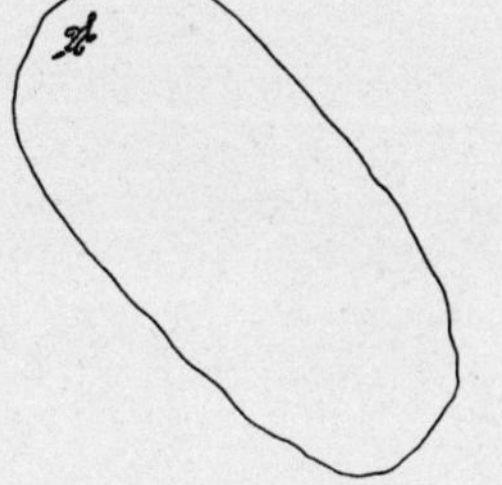

098 At last: oval tomatoes.

No wheels – no bike.

OHNE RAD KEIN RAD.

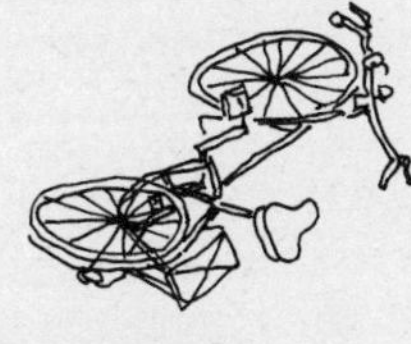

JUNGER APFEL.

ALTER APFEL.

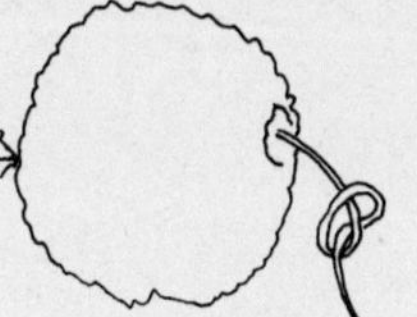

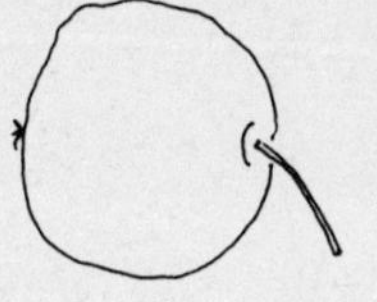

Young apple. Old apple.

Like an open book.

SO WIE EIN OFFENES BUCH.

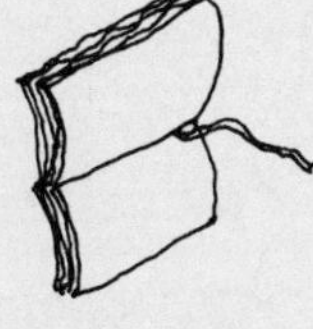

SEHR
BEQUEM.

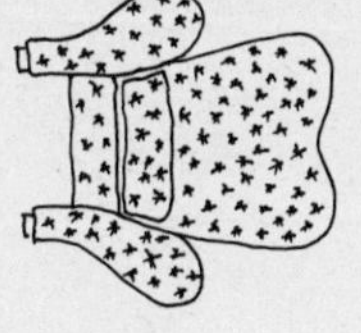

Very comfy.

Rice on the floor.

REIS AM BODEN.

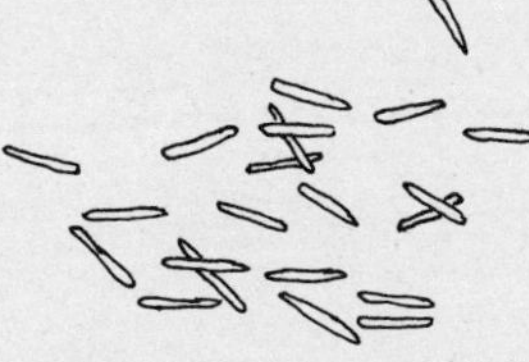

TAGEBUCH
DES
REISES.

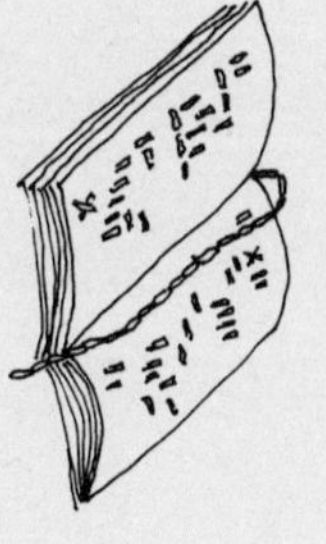

Rice diary.

Tall man.

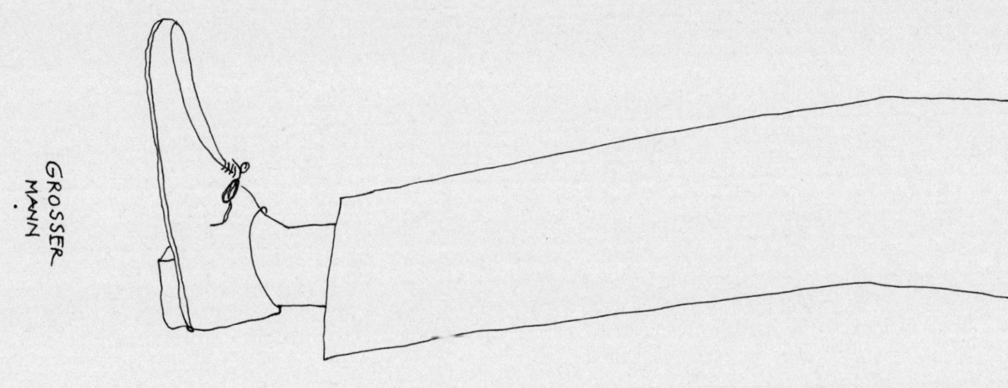

HERZ

:

OPTIMIERT

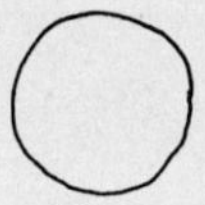

.

Heart. Optimised.

Hankies have stories to tell.

TASCHENTÜCHER
KÖNNEN
VIEL
ERZÄHLEN.

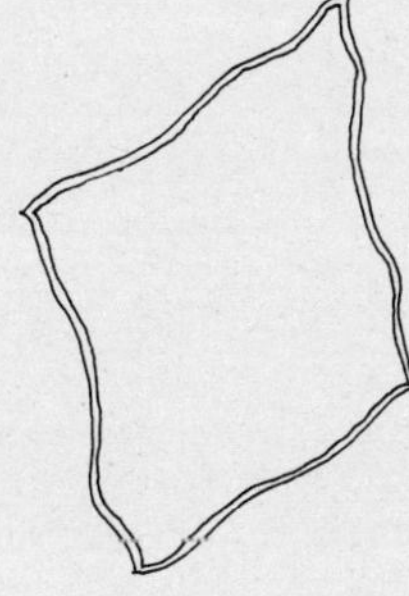

VERKEHRT
AM
KOPF.

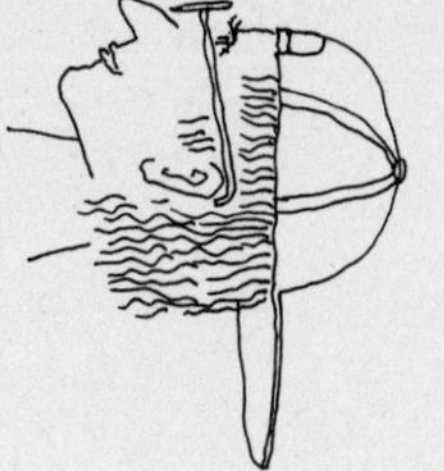

Everyone always smiles.

ALLE
LÄCHELN
IMMER.

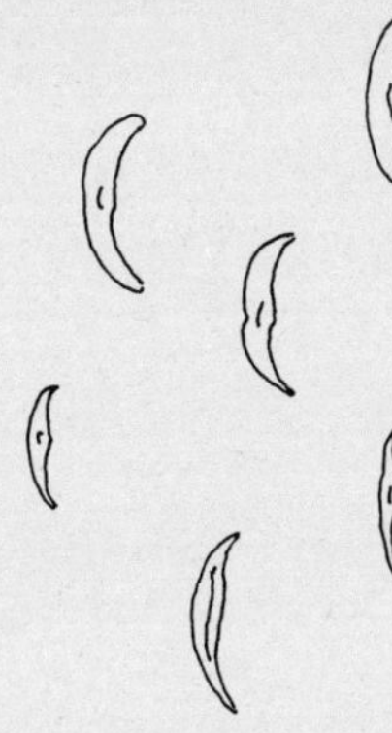

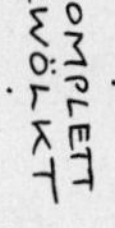

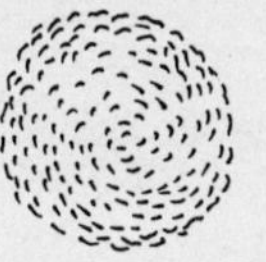

The earth. Completely clouded over.

Been through too much.

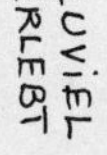

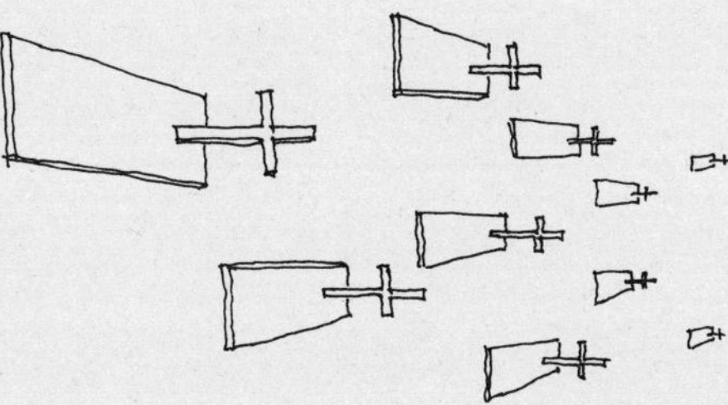

SCHNEE
SCHAUFEL
GERÄUSCHE.

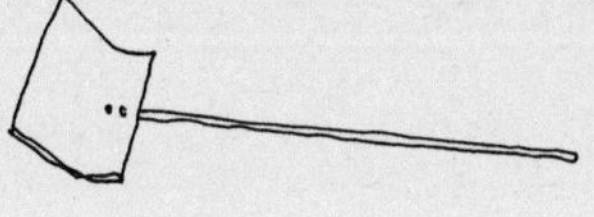

The sound of the snow shovel.

Heavy world view.

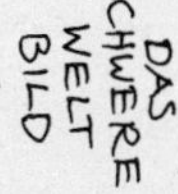

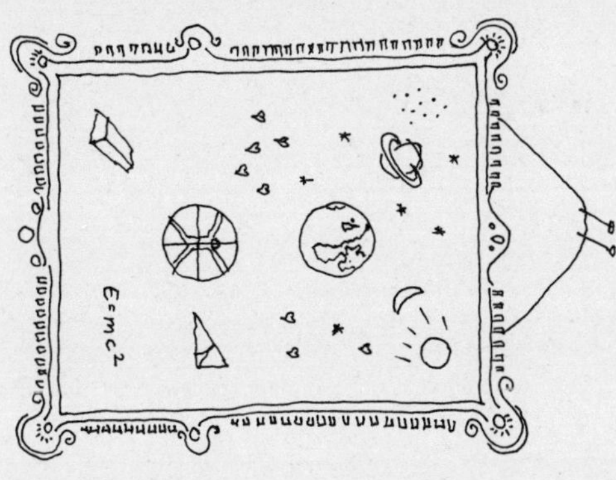

DAS
LEICHTE
WELT
BILD
.

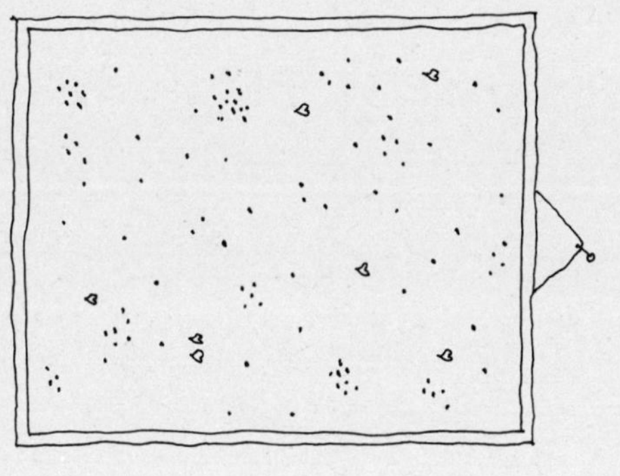

Light world view.

A timid heart.

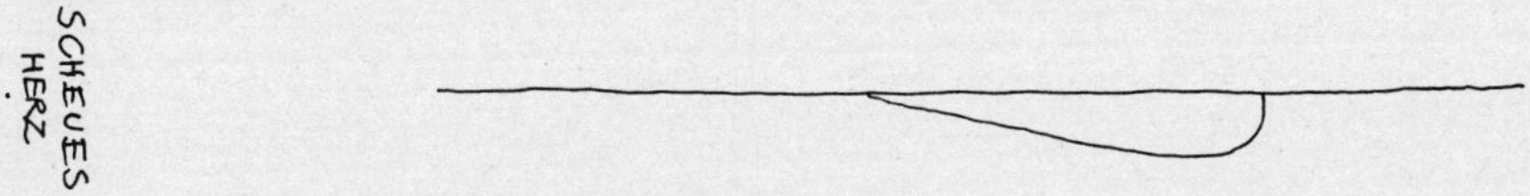

SCHEUES HERZ.

HERZEN
UNTER
EINER
DECKE.

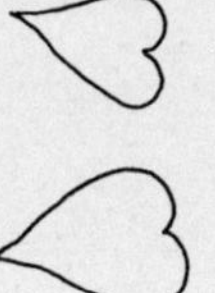

Hearts under one blanket.

Power over dogs.

MACHT
ÜBER
HUNDE.

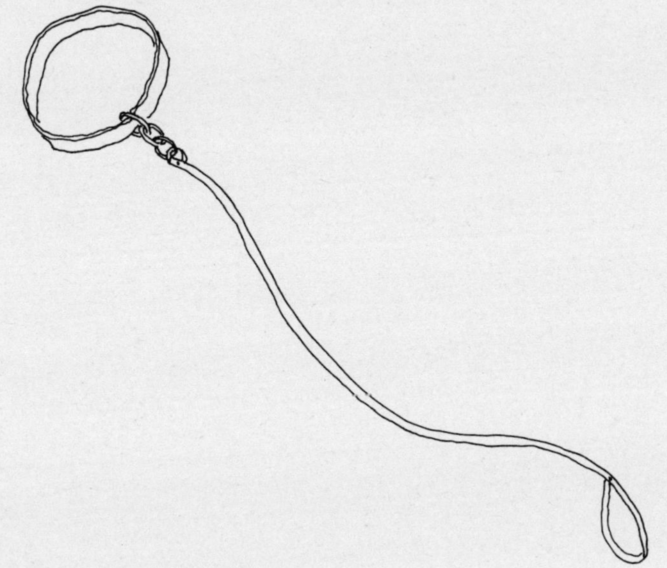

BÜCHER
SCHREIBT
MAN
AUCH
SELBER.

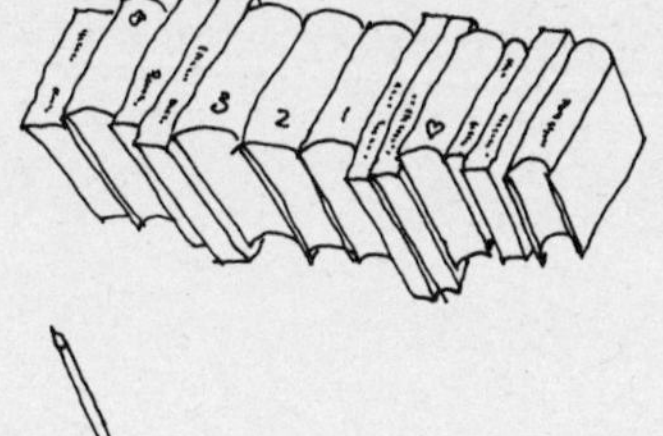

Any of these a book you wrote yourself?

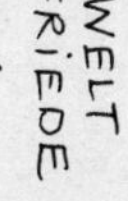
WELT
FRIEDE.

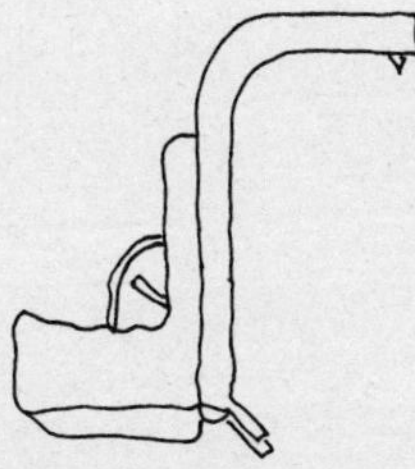

GESTERN
WAR
ALLES
SO
KLAR.

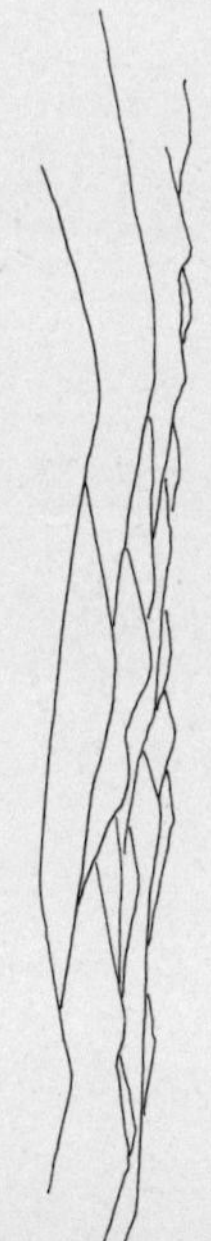

Yesterday, everything was so clear.

Who invented parmesan? Signor Spaghetti!

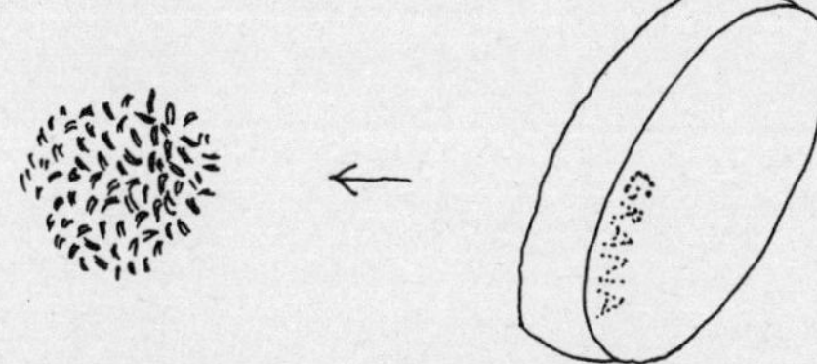

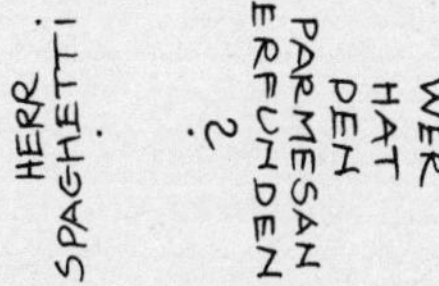

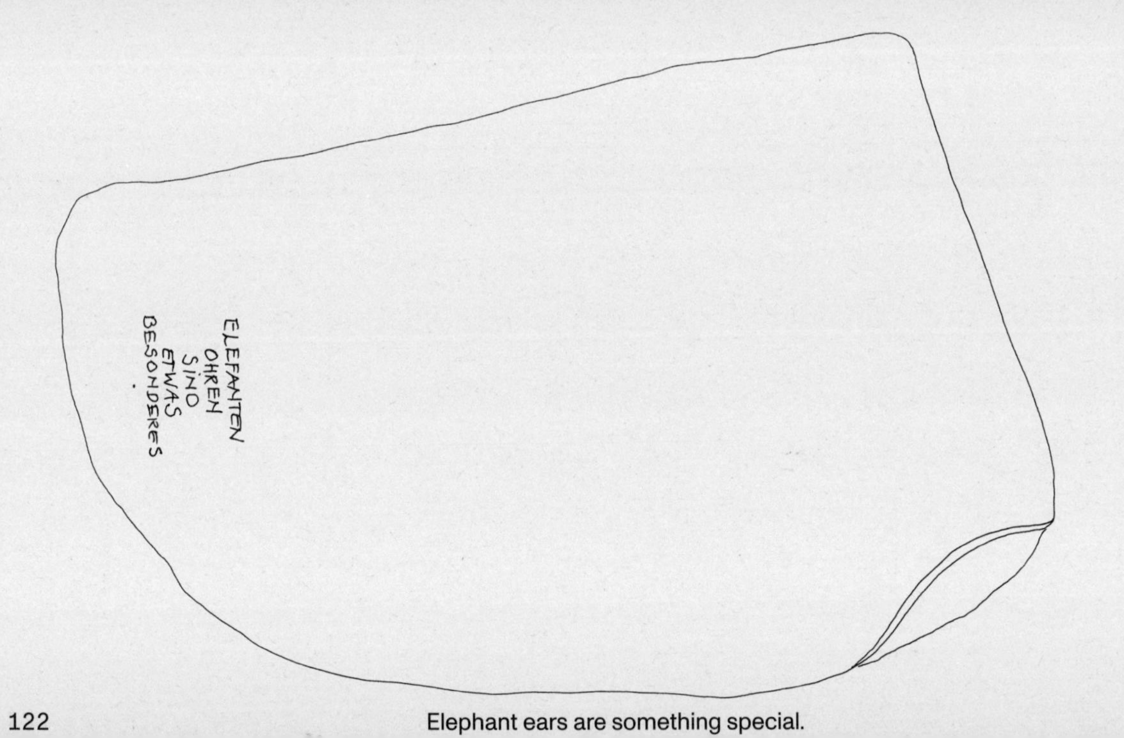

Elephant ears are something special.

For life.

LEBENS
LANG.

DIE
AMEISENKÖNIGIN
MIT
GROSSER
KRONE.

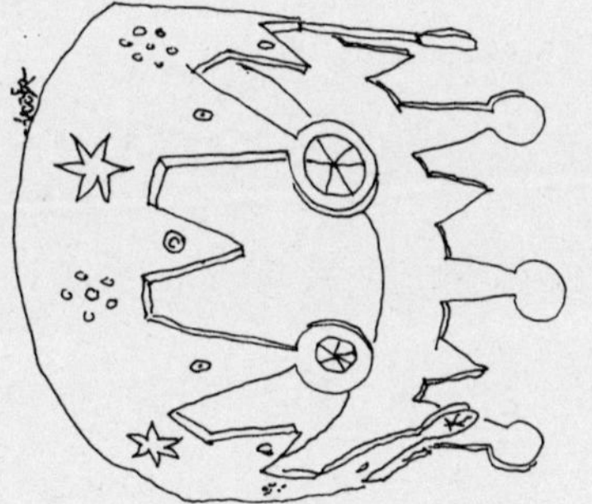

The queen ant with a big crown.

The conductor's chopsticks.

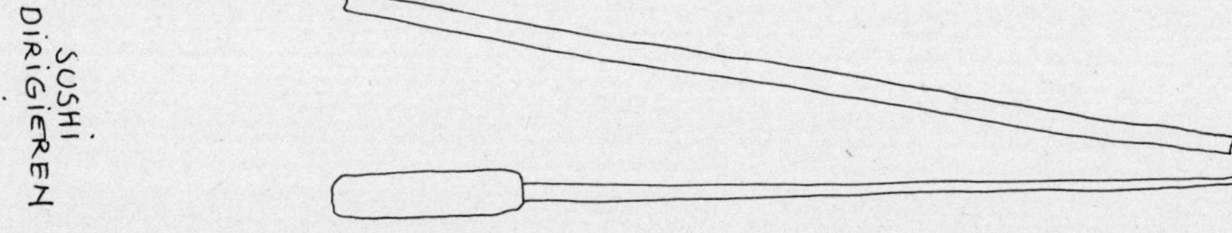

ERSTES
HAAR.

First hair.

First shame.

ERSTE SCHAM.

KEINE
GARANTIE.

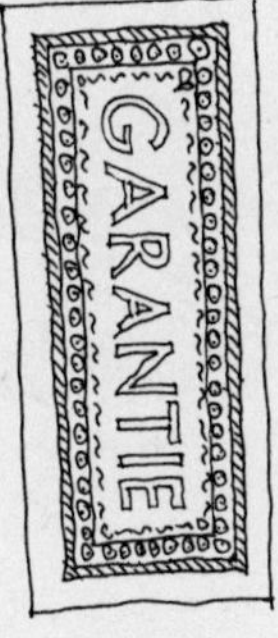

No guarantee.

A Brit is as stiff as a stick.

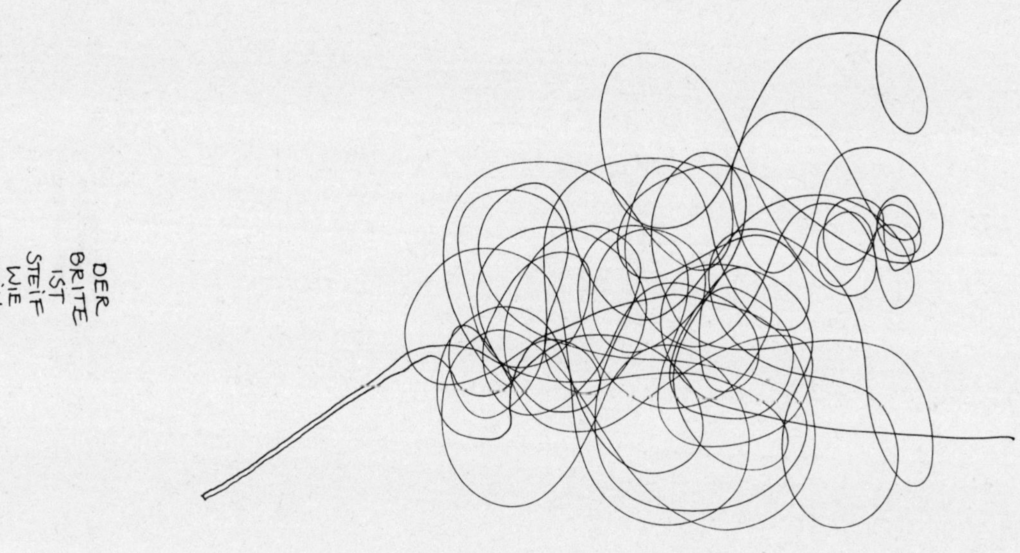

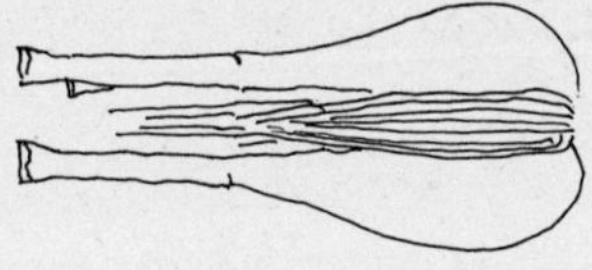

PFERDE
SCHLAFEN
IM
STEHEN
.

Horses sleep on their feet.

Tree without fruit.

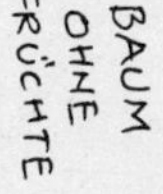

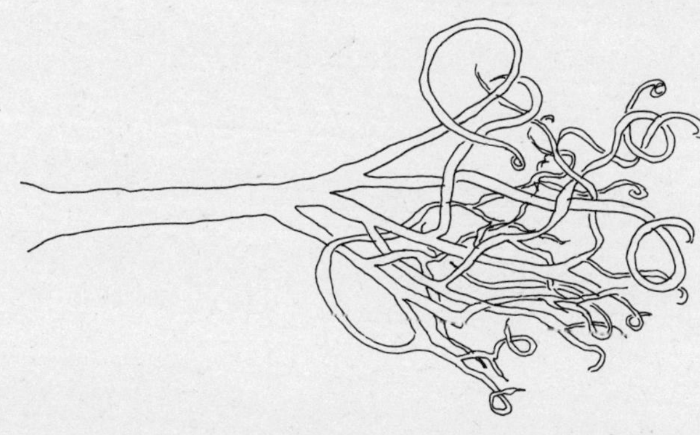

DAS
LEBEN
BERÜHREN.

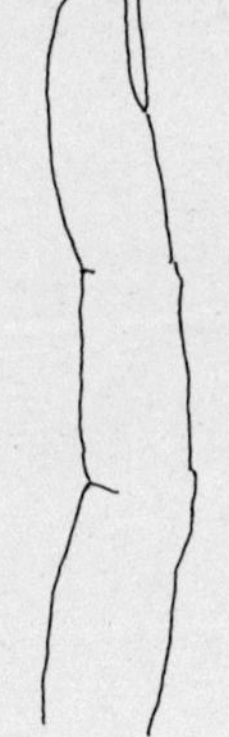

In touch with life.

The other day, the medicine man had an absurd idea.

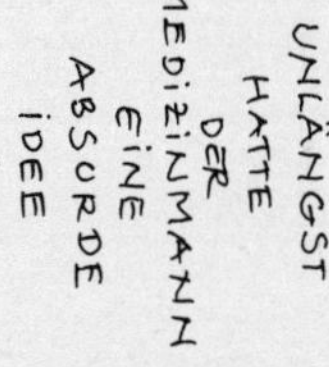

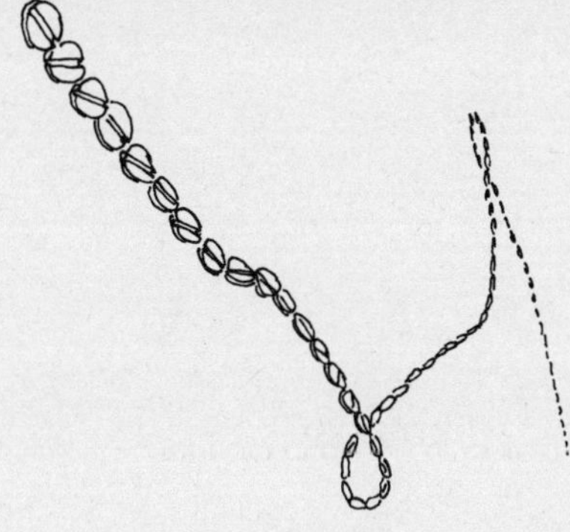

WIE
WEGGEBLASEN.

Gone in the blink of an eye.

Spirits of life.

LEBENS
GEISTER

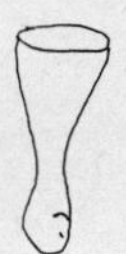

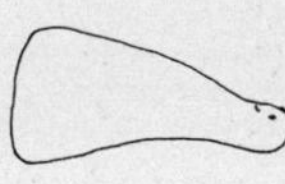

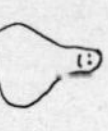

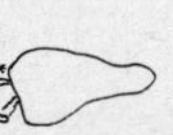

HÖHEPUNKTE.

High points.

Having made it to the top.

OBEN ANGEKOMMEN.

NIEMAND
WILL
SO
AUSSEHEN
WIE
GIACOMETTI'S.

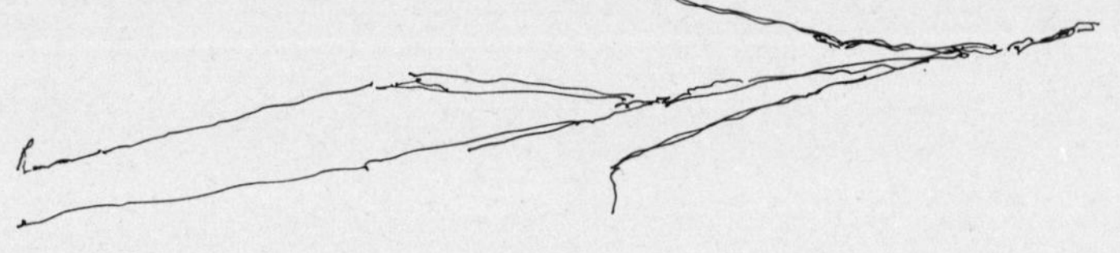

No one wants that Giacometti look for themselves.

A national border?

LANDES
GRENZE
?

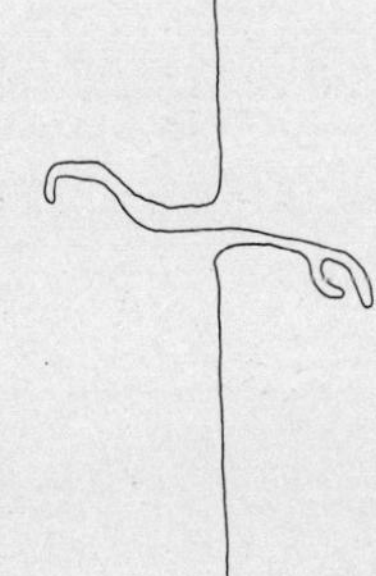

NICHTS
UNENDLICH
VERGRÖSSERT
.

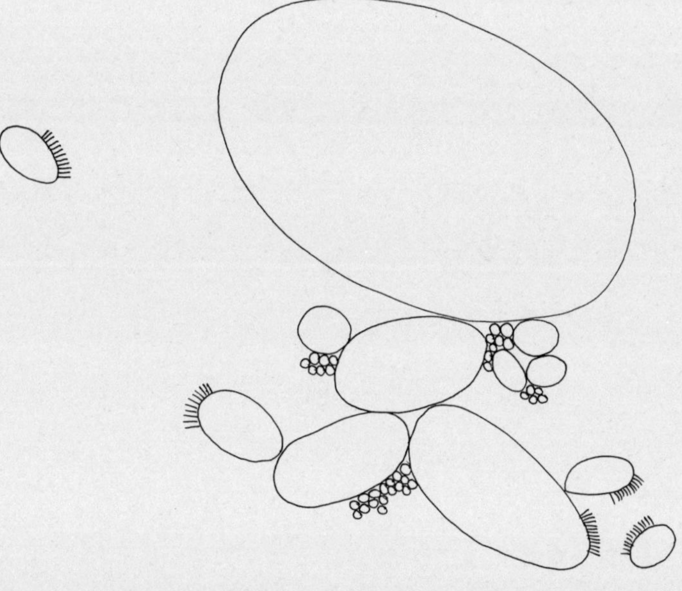

Nothing, infinitely magnified.

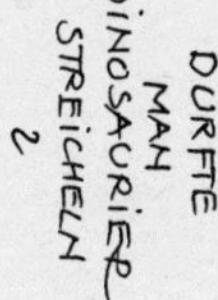
DURFTE
MAN
DINOSAURIER
STREICHELN
?

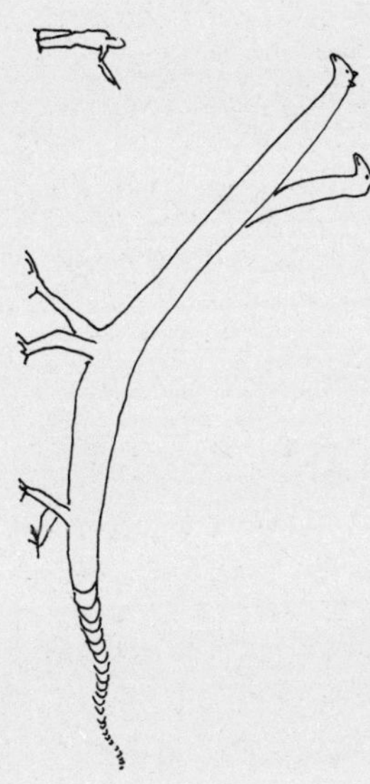

VIELLEICHT
WAR
ICH
FRÜHER
EINE
WASSERMELONE
.

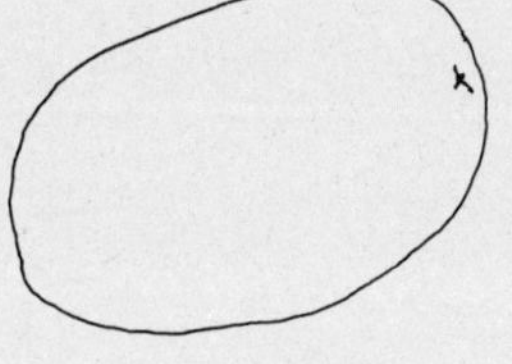

 There was perhaps a time when I was a water melon.

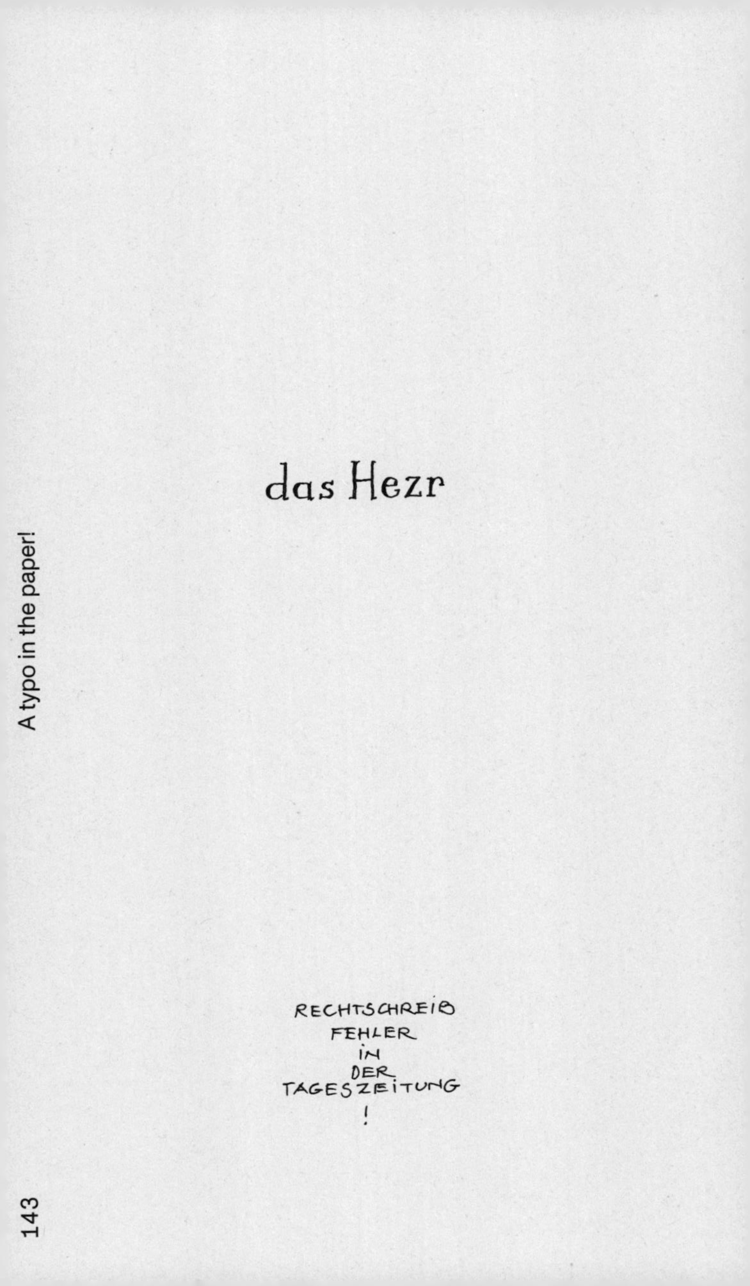

das Hezr

RECHTSCHREIB
FEHLER
IN
DER
TAGESZEITUNG
!

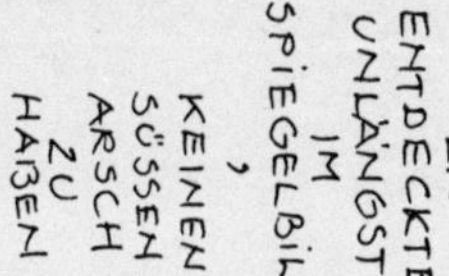

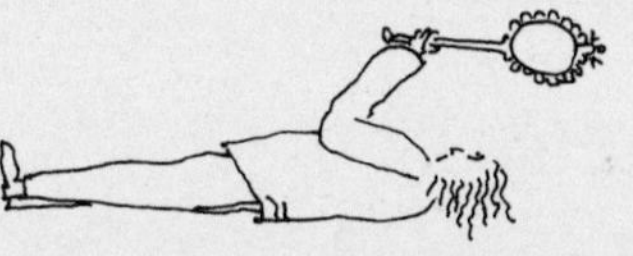

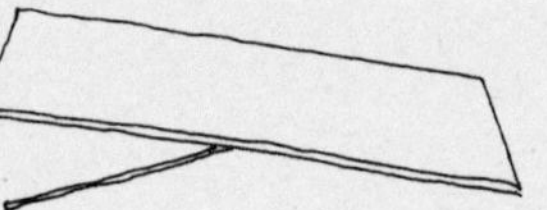

The other day, he discovered in the mirror that he didn't have a sexy butt.

Love manual for robots.

LIEBESANLEITUNG
FÜR
ROBOTER.

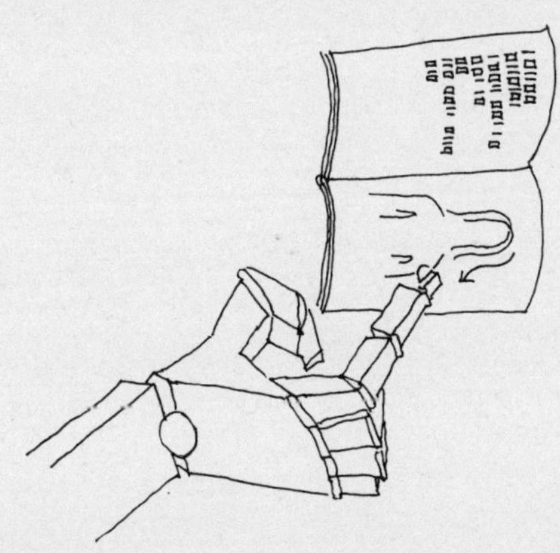

DAS
ANDERE
ENDE.

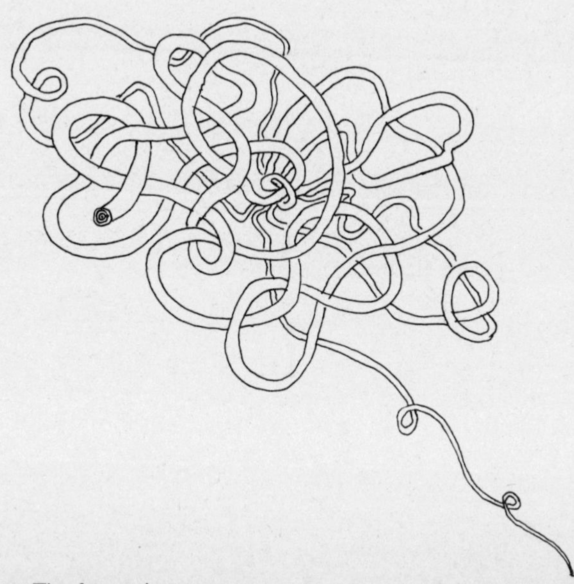

The far end.

147

A sea of birds.

EIN
VOGELMEER.

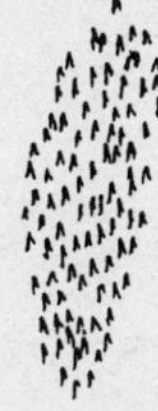

ERFINDER
JONATHAN
ASS
ALS
ERSTER
MENSCH
EIN
TIER.

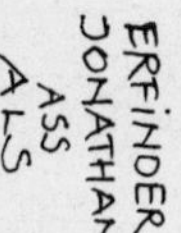

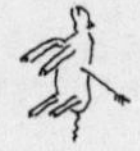

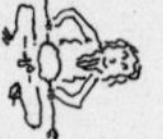

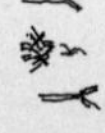

Inventor Jonathan was the first person to eat an animal.

Unusual: a bird affected by a fear of flying.

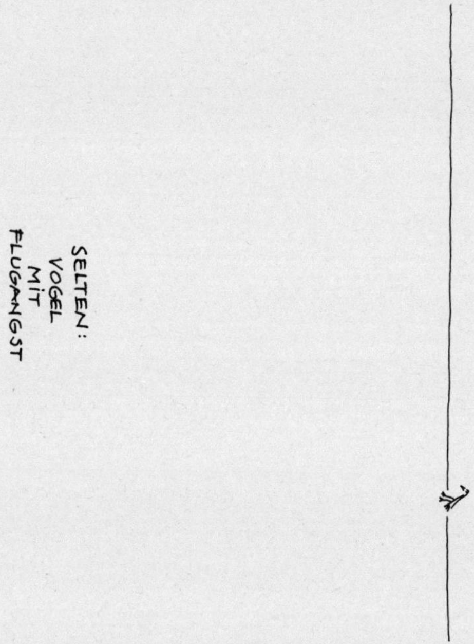

SELTEN:
VOGEL
MIT
FLUGANGST.

SONNENBRILLE
IM
WINTER
SCHLAF
.

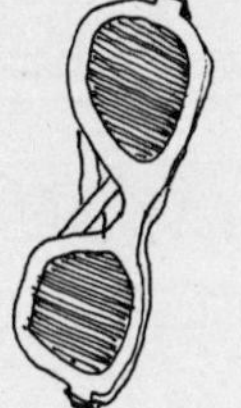

Sunglasses in hibernation mode.

Learning to live.

LEBEN
LERNEN

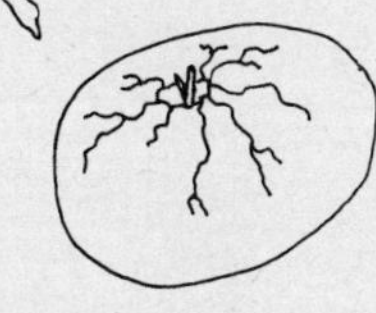

TRAUER
PHASEN.

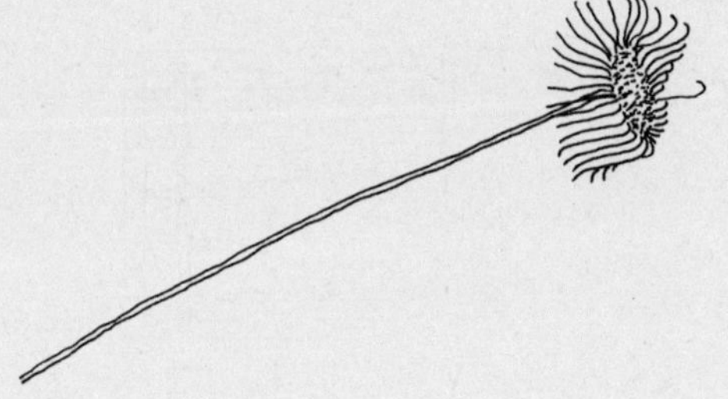

Phases of mourning.

Making a run for it.

AUSGEBROCHEN

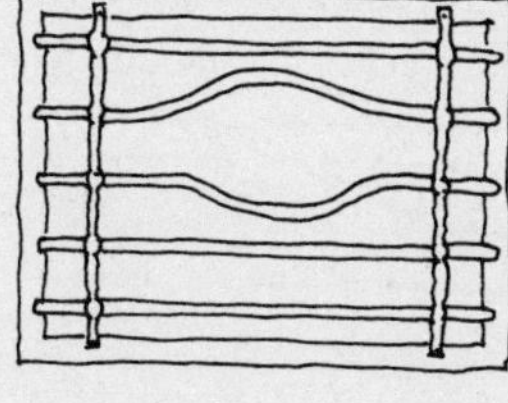

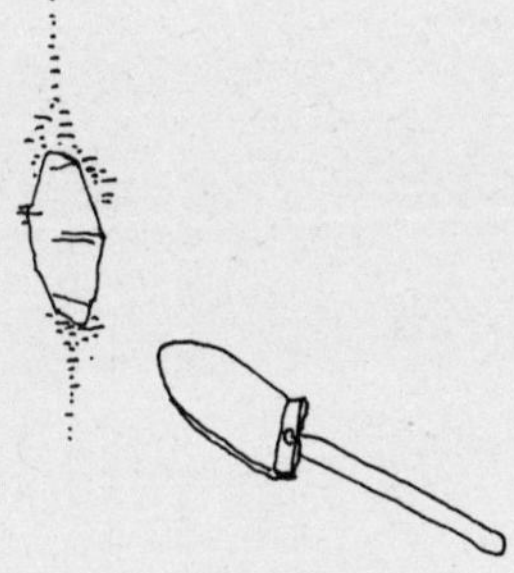

Plants transplanted.

In conference with the ocean.

BESPRECHUNG
MIT
DEM
OZEAN.

DER
DICKE,
GEMÜTLICHE
BAUM.

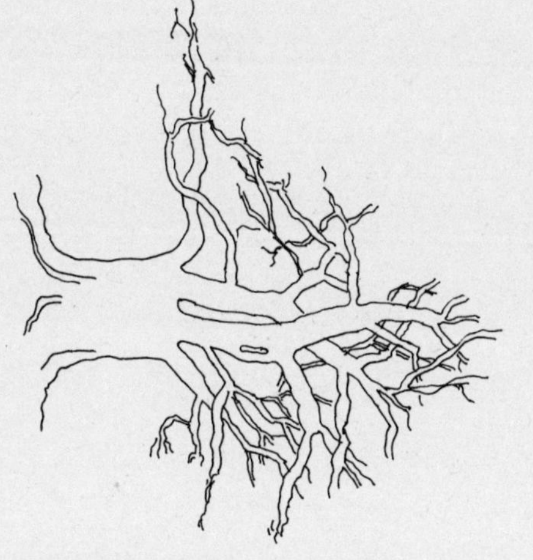

Big tree, taking it easy.

The largest tear on record.

GRÖSSTE JE GEMESSENE TRÄNE.

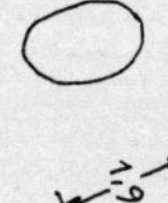

ELEFANTEN
TRÄNEN.

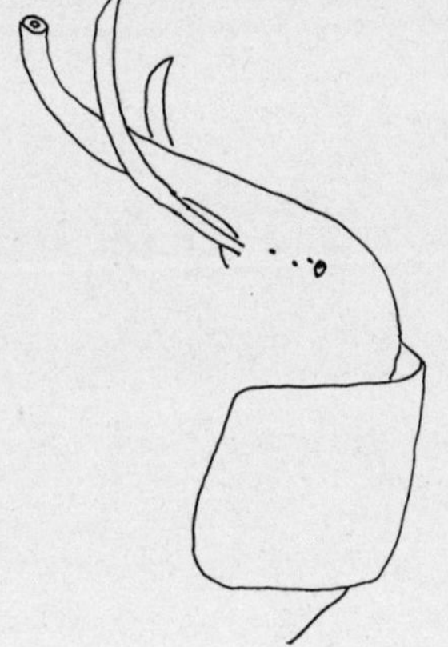

 Elephant tears.

James Bond for Christmas.

JAMES
BOND
ZUR
WEIHNACHTS
ZEIT
.

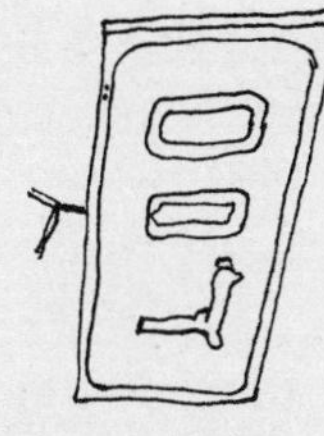

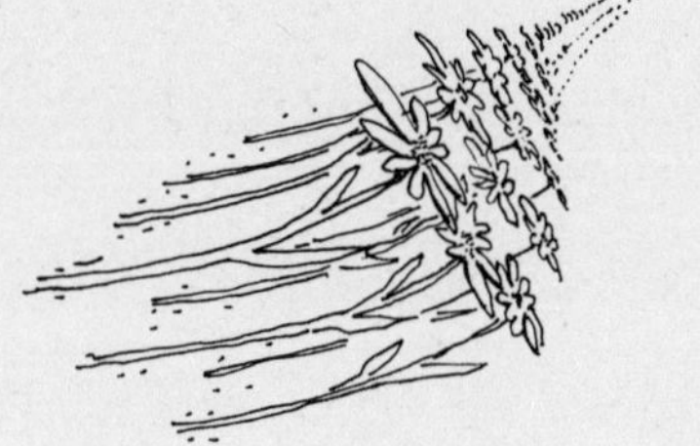

WACHSTUMS
STREIK
IM
GEWÄCHS
HAUS.

Growth strike in the greenhouse.

A lot of kindly spirits in the luggage.

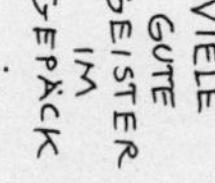

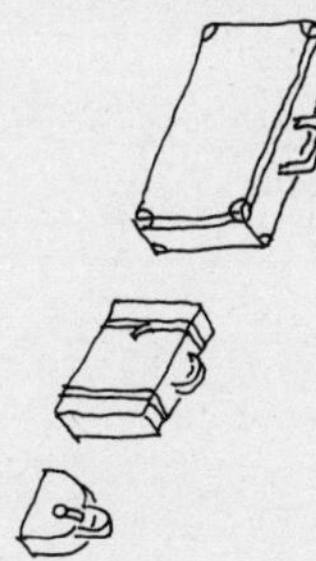

ALLE
MEN SCHEN
SCHLAFEN
NACHTS
.

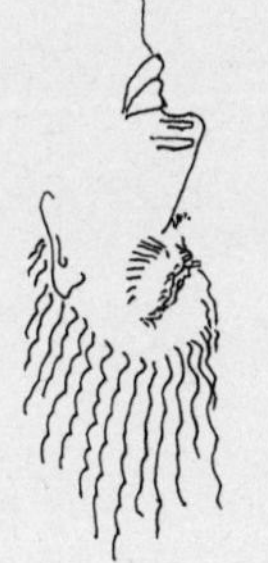

Everyone sleeps at night.

Is it true that in your lifetime you eat a supermarket's worth of food?

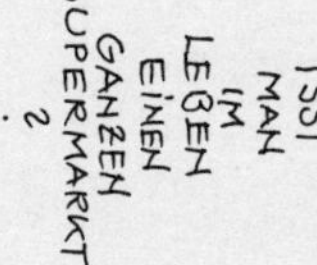

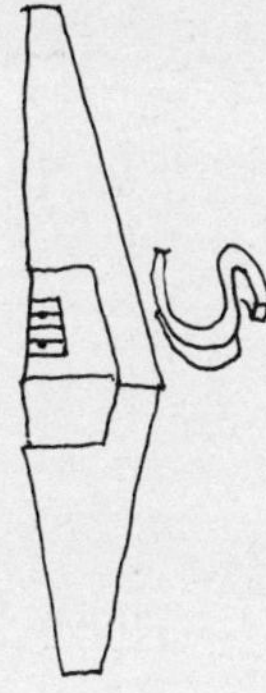

DER
SCHALK
IM
AUGE.

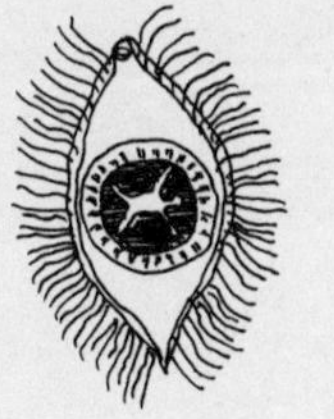

A roguish twinkle in the eye.

Three minutes of brushing your teeth cannot be shortened.

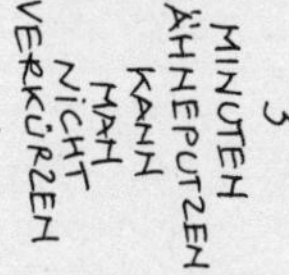

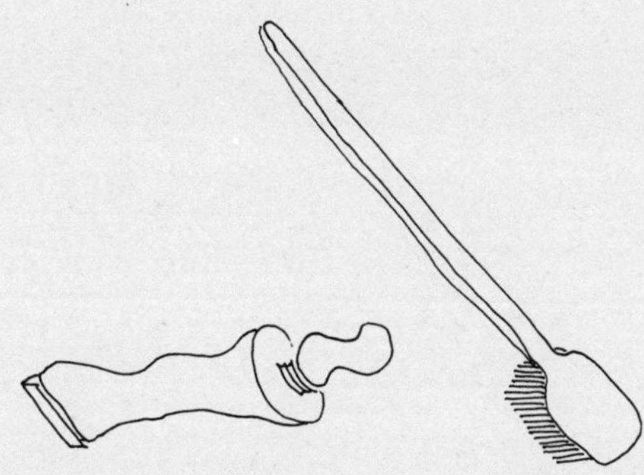

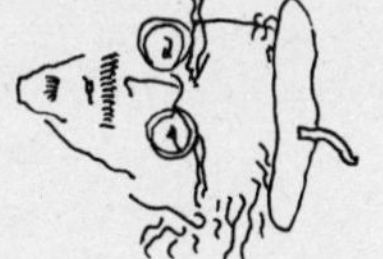

FRANÇOIS . DER BESTE .

François. The bee’s knees.

Food to delight the polar bear.

ESSENS
FREUDE
BEIM
EISBÄREN

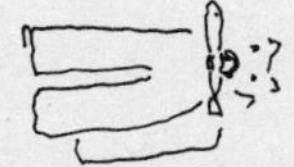

DER
VOGEL
ERFAND
DAS
FLIEGEN.

Birds invented flight.

Banana, measured.

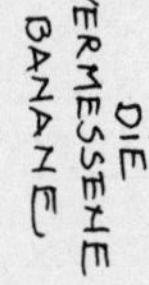

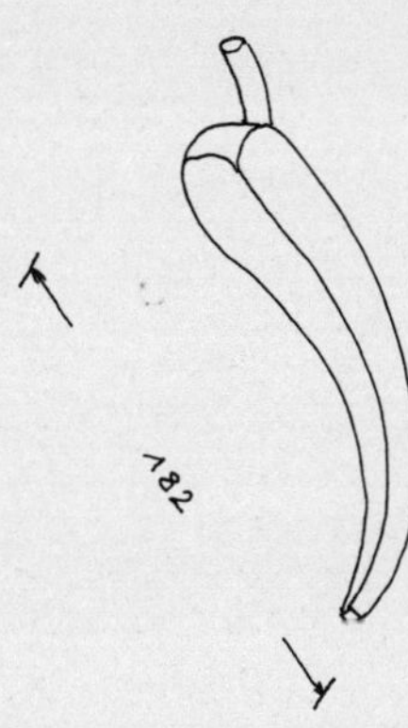

DIE
ZWEITE
PISTAZIE.

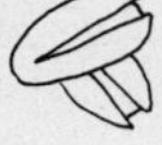

The second pistachio.

The forbidden mountain of whipped cream.

DER
VERBOTENE
SAHNE
BERG

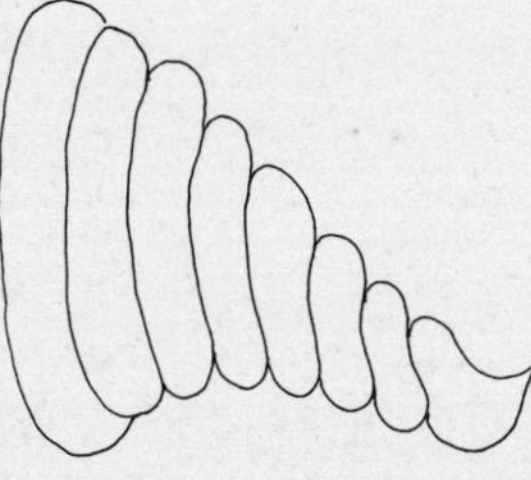

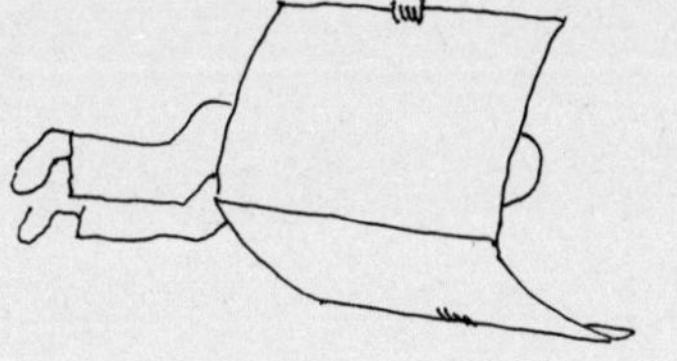

Taking time out.

Hearing the needle drop.

DIE
STECK
NADEL
FALLEN
HÖREN.

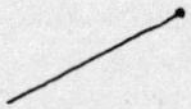

DIE
SCHÖNSTE
BLUME
VERPACKT

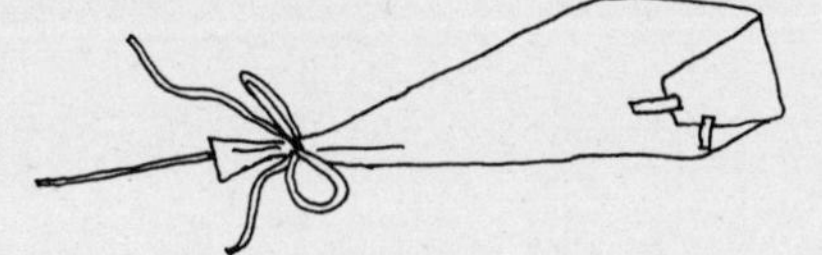

The most beautiful flower. Wrapped.

Sick doctor. Self-fulfilling prophecy?

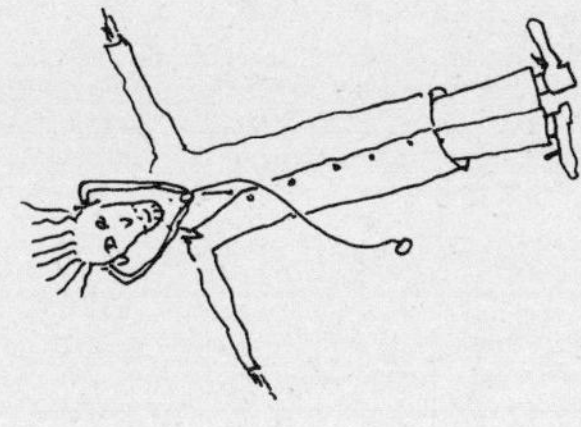

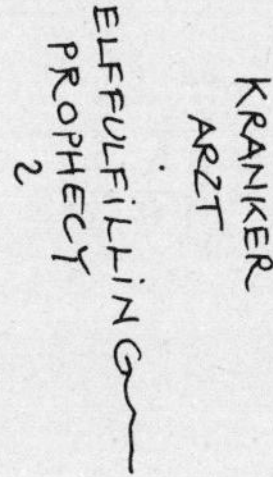

WAS
KANN
AN
EINEM
FISCH
SCHON
FALSCH
SEIN
?

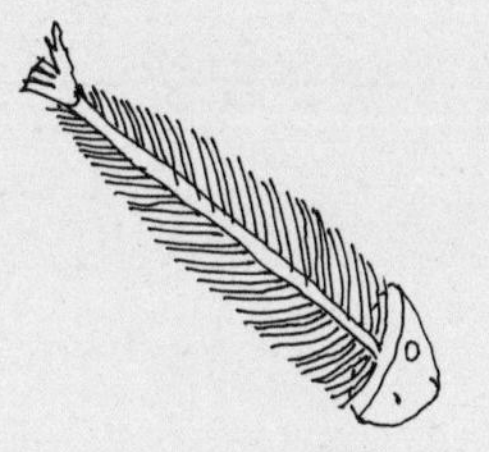

What can possibly go wrong with a fish?

The picture touched me.

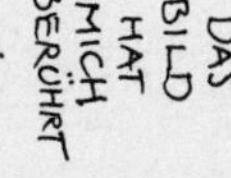

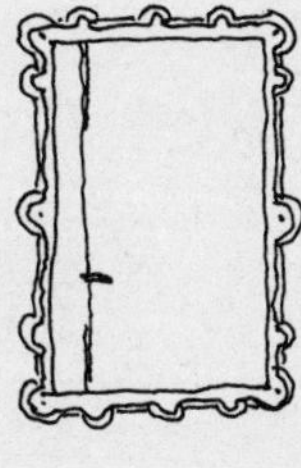

SELBSTWACHSENDES
PFLÄNZCHEN.

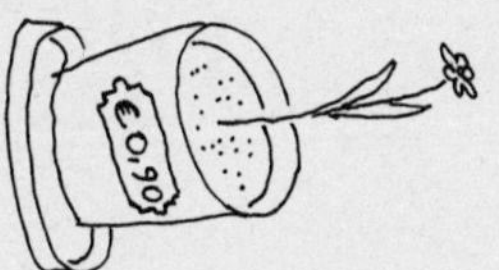

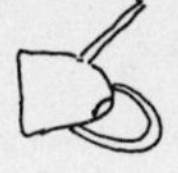

Self-growing seedling.

Exhibition at the Egg School. 3rd semester.

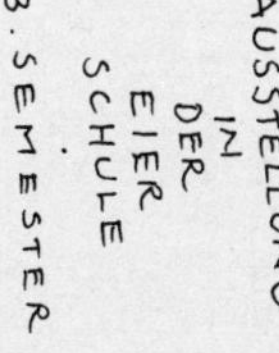

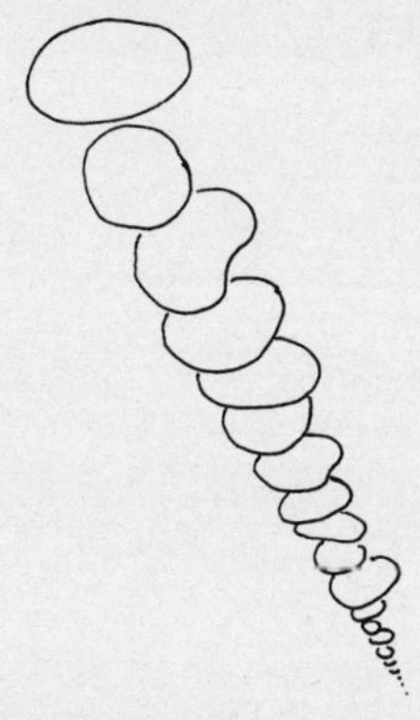

DAS
FELL
DES
DESIGNERHUNDES.

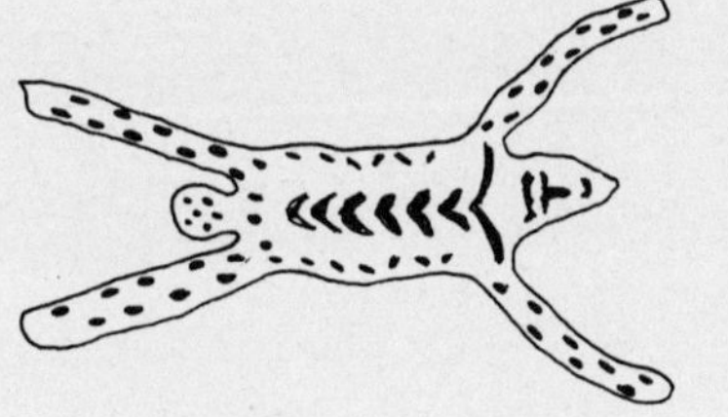

The skin of the designer dog.

BACH
FORELLE
IM
OZEAN

RESPEKT.

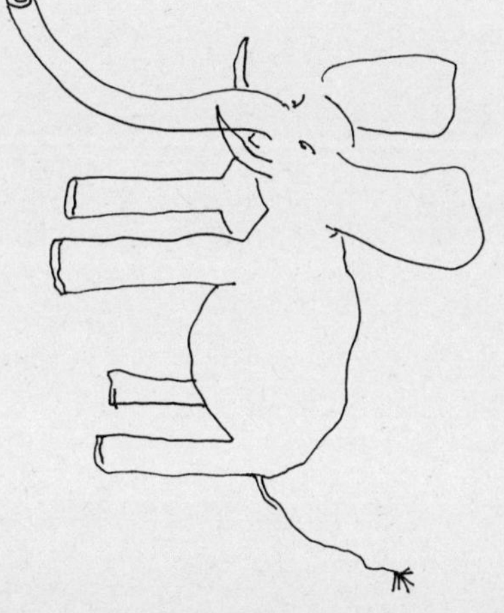

Respect!

Small head. Capacious mind.

KLEINER KOPF, GROSSER GEIST.

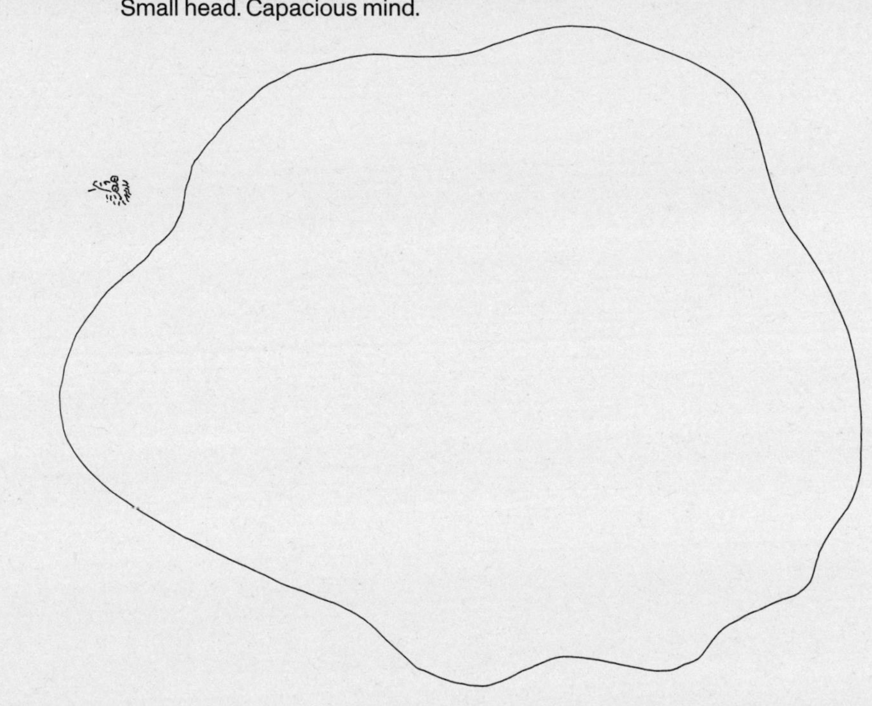

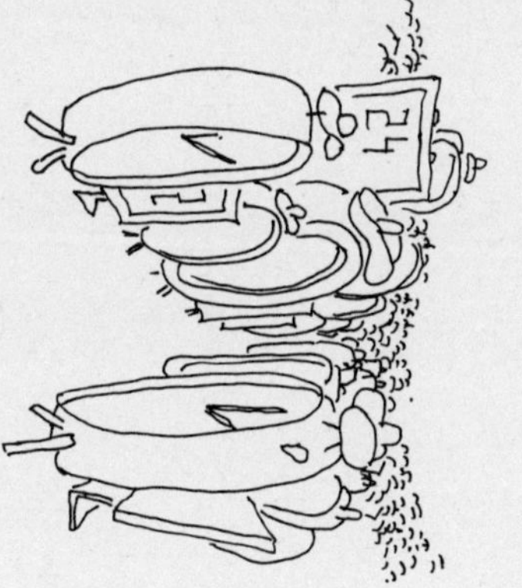

The city of perpetual alarm clocks.

DER
UNZUFRIEDENE
TOURISTEN
ARSCH
.

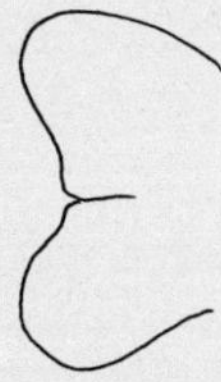

SCHARFES
LEBEN.

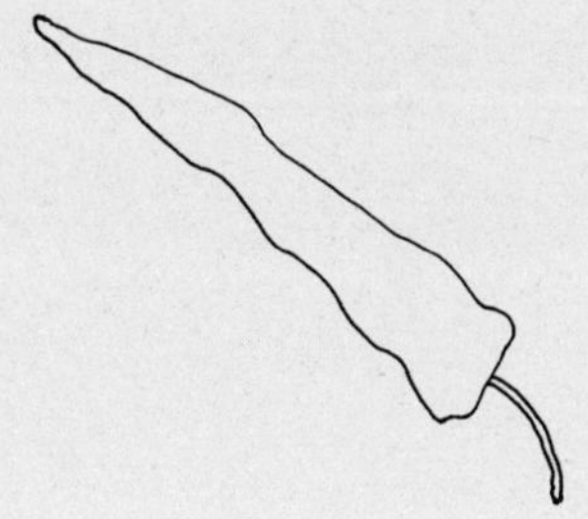

Hot life.

AUGEN

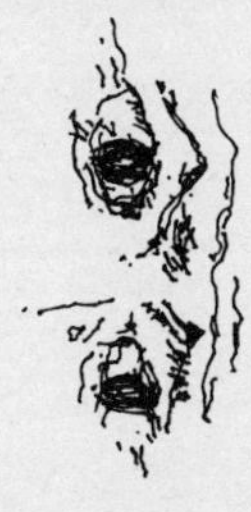

ELEFANT
UND
SEINE
SCHWESTER
.

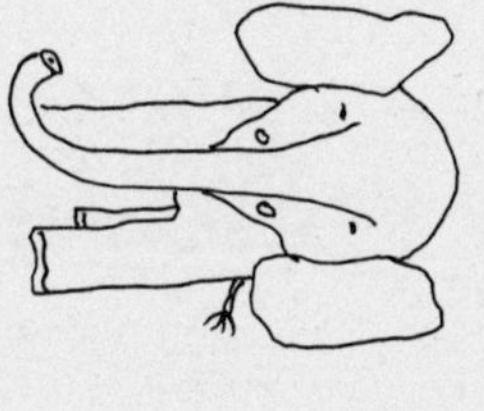

The elephant and his sister.

ANDERE SPRACHE.

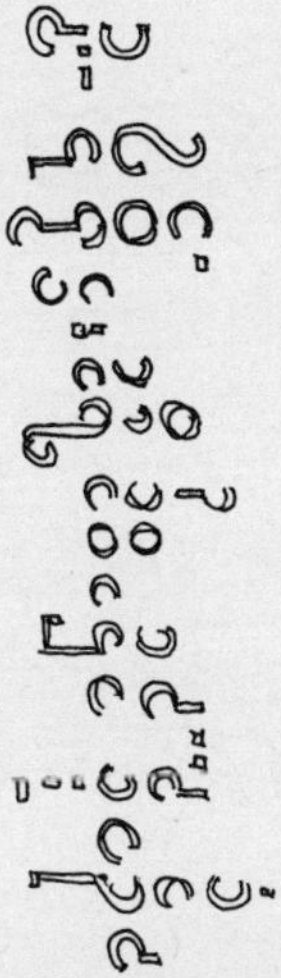

DICKE
HAUT.

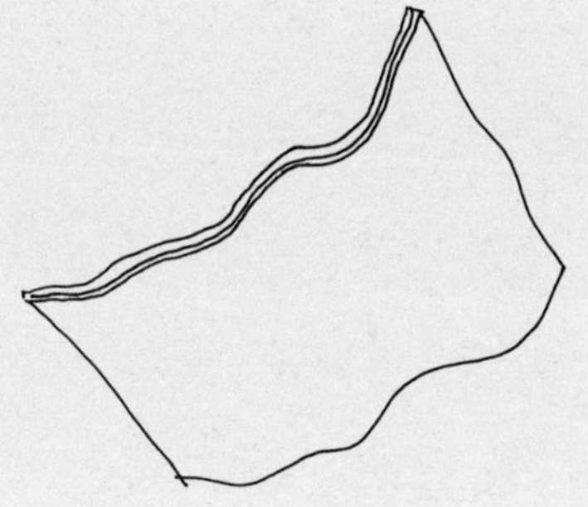

Thick skin.

The responsibility of the American President.

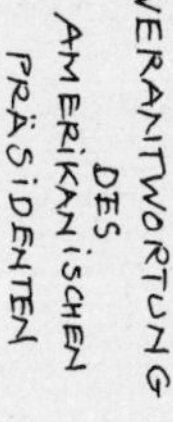

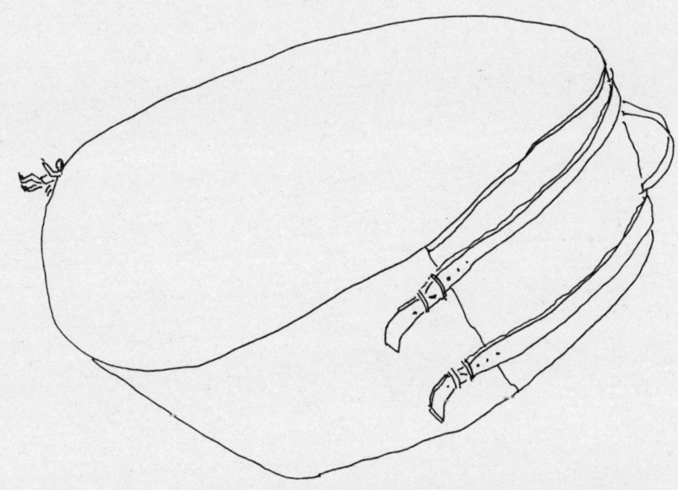

MASSLOS
ZUCKER.

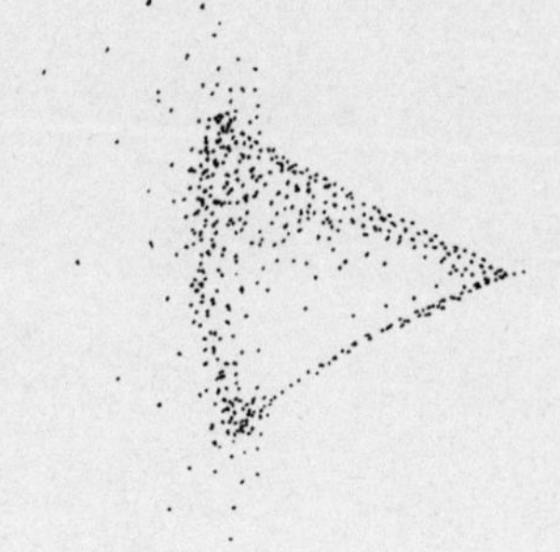

Sugar unlimited.

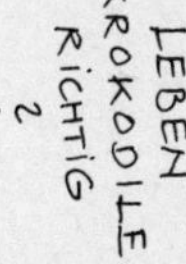
LEBEN
KROKODILE
RICHTIG
?

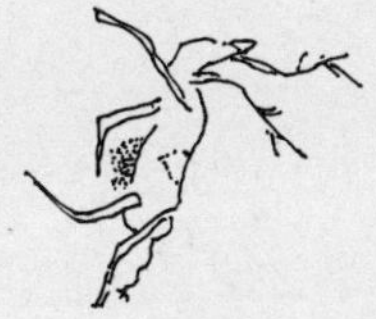

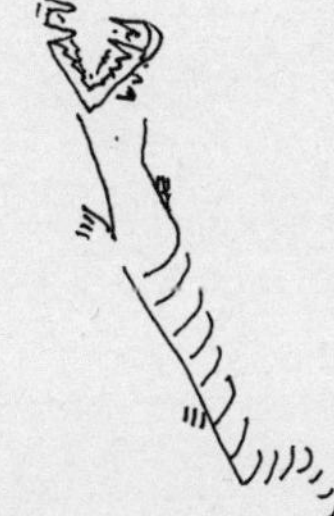

HOLZ
MACHT
MUSIK.

Wood makes music.

WO
IST
DAS
HERZ
IM
BAUM
?

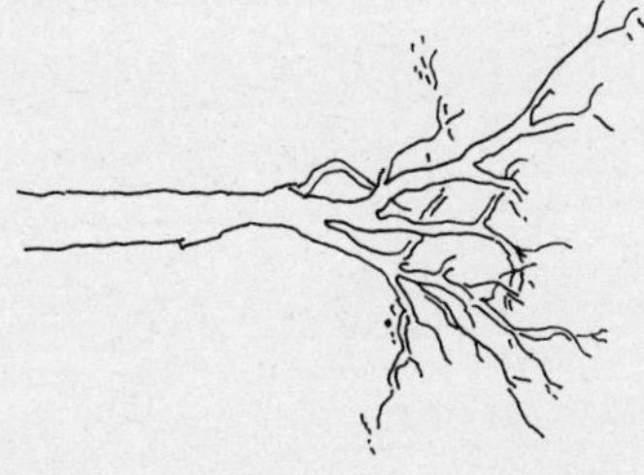

EINTAGSFLIEGE
AM
WEG
ZUM
MOND.

A mayfly on its way to the moon.

MENSCH
ÄRGERE
DICH
NICHT
.
VATER
&
SOHN

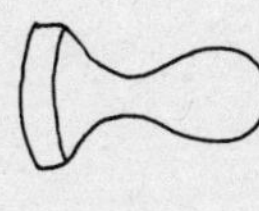

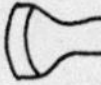

MINI
ROCK.

Miniskirt.

Order.

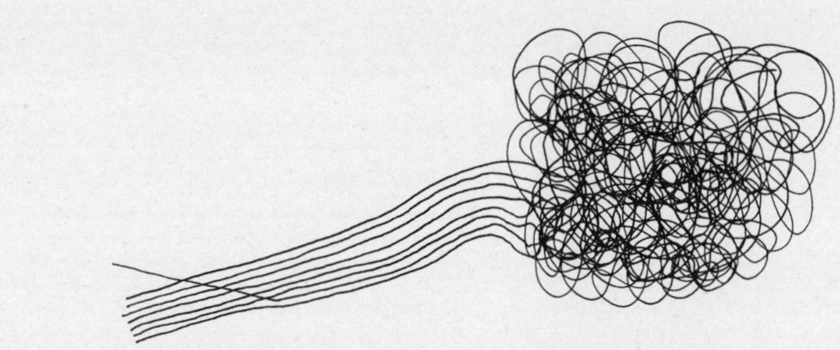

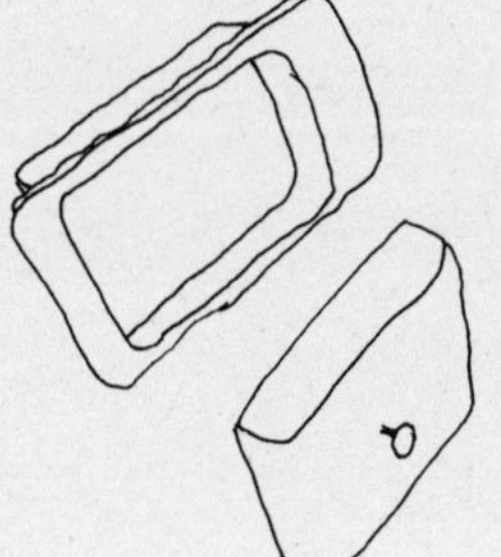

The butter dish. A highly controversial invention.

A mountain built exclusively from sand.

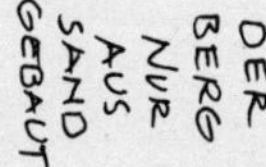

GANZES
KIND.

An entire child.

Did presidents use to love gummy bears?

LIEBTEN
PRÄSIDENTEN
FRÜHER
GUMMIBÄREN
?

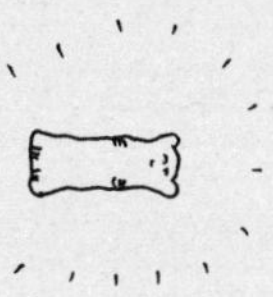

VERKEHRTE ZEIT.

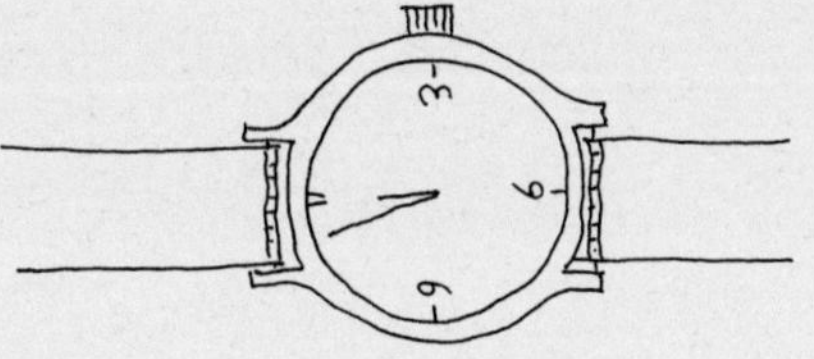

Time gone haywire.

Passing on the treasure.

DEN
SCHATZ
WEITERGEBEN.

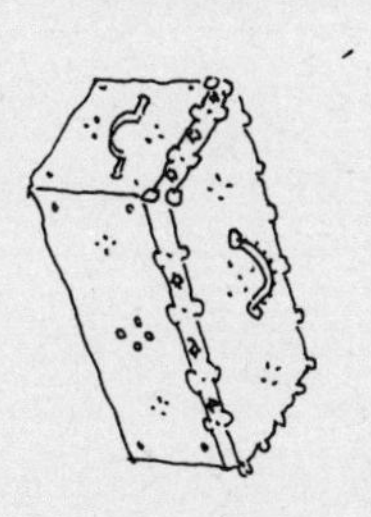

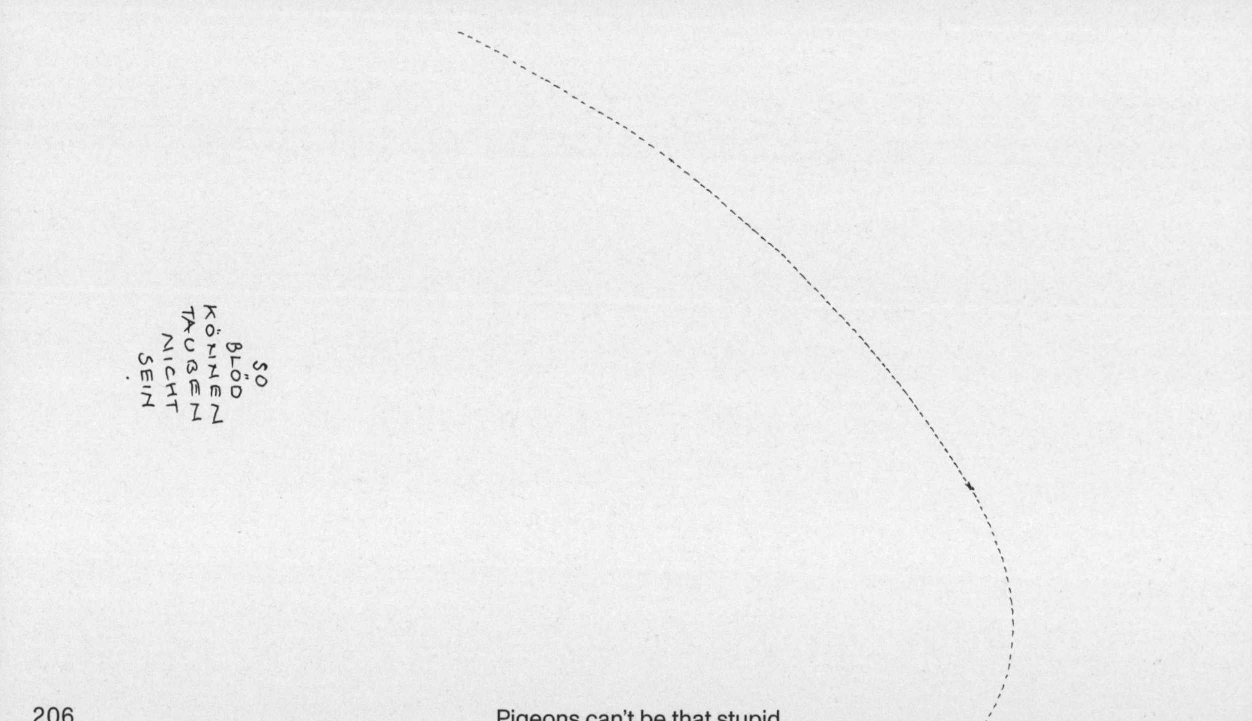

Pigeons can't be that stupid.

LEBENS
WERK

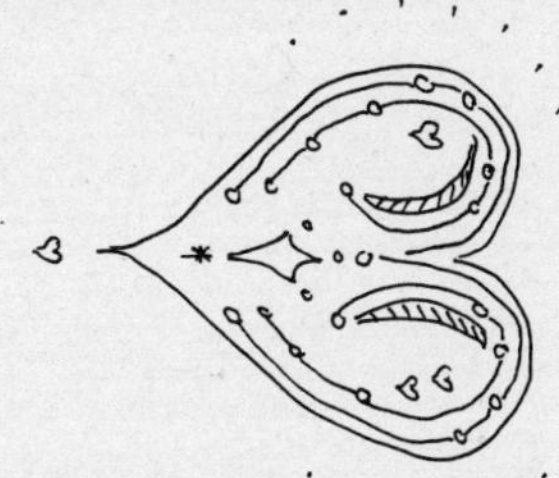

FISCHE
BRAUCHEN
KEINE
HÄNDE.

Fish have no need for hands.

The best corn kernel on the cob.

DAS
BESTE
KORN
IM
MAISKOLBEN.

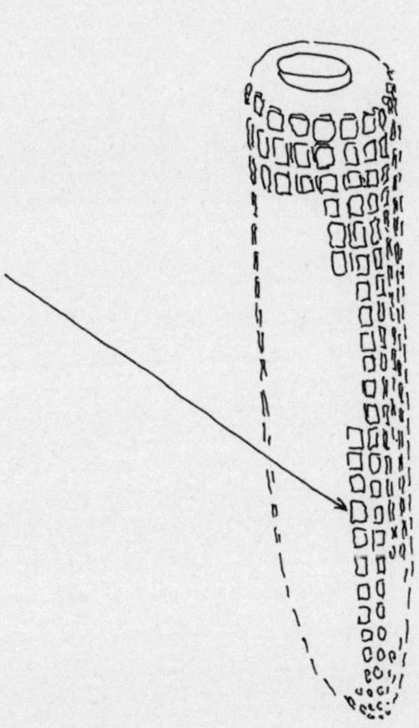

WEGGESCHAUT

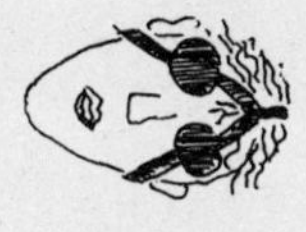

Looking away.

The unshorn sheep.

DAS
UNGESCHORENE
SCHAF

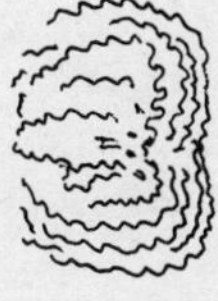

NEU
:
FENSTER
IM
FLUGZEUGTOILETTEN
.

New: Windows in airplane toilets.

A whim of nature. Uncut diamond.

UN
GESCHLIFFENER
DIAMANT
.

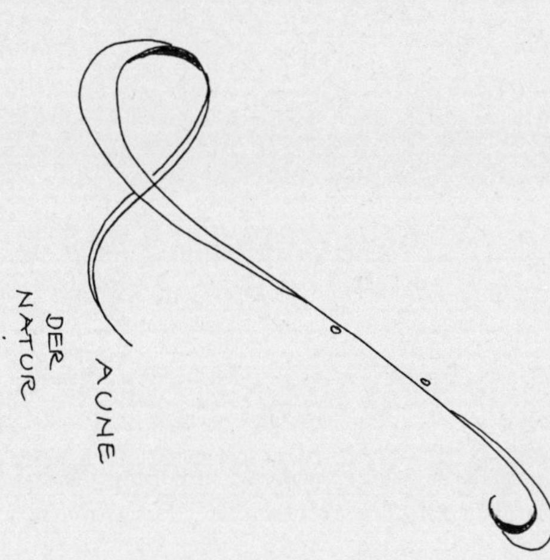

ICH
KENNE
ALLE
MEINE
JEANS.
PERSÖNLICH

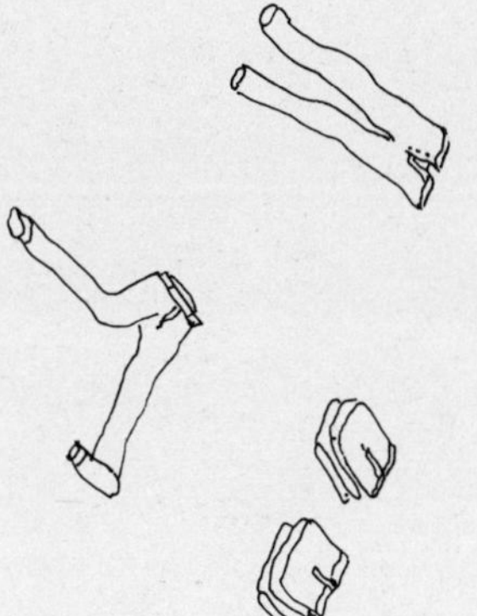

I am on an intimate footing with all my jeans.

Two tired warriors. Greatly reduced in size.

ZWEI
MÜDE
KRIEGER
.
STARK
VERKLEINERT
.

AUF
DER
WAAGE
ZIEHT
ER
IMMER
DEN
BAUCH
EIN.

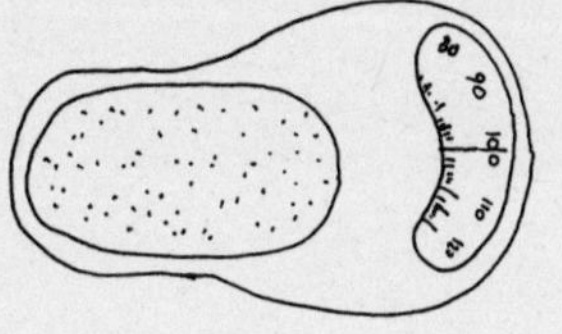

On the scales he always draws in his stomach.

DER GEFALLENE WÜRFEL.

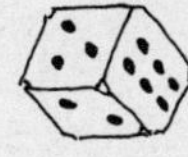

EIN
KLEINER
SCHRITT.

A small step.

Three grains of sand and an ocean.

3
SANDKÖRNER
UND
EIN
OZEAN.

FRAU
KOMPOTT.

Mrs Compote.

Your own cabbage.

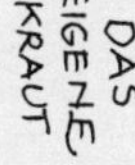

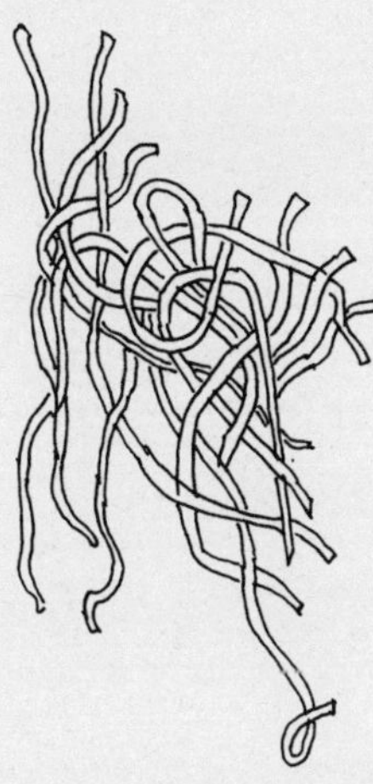

DIE
WELTFORMEL
ENTHÄLT
EINE
WURZEL.

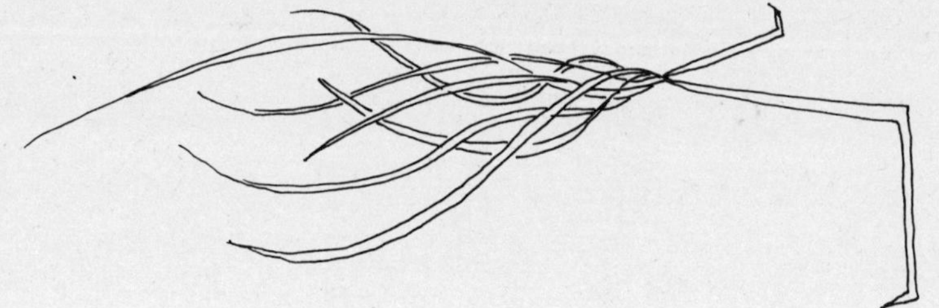

The theory of everything comprises a root.

Cap of invisibility, model FBI.

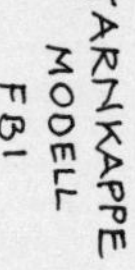

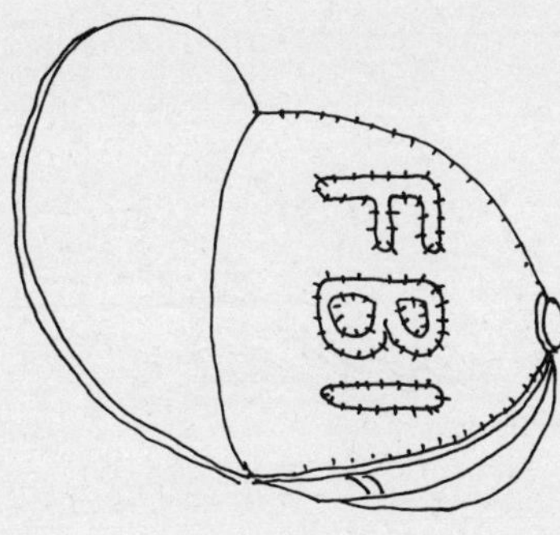

FREMDES
HAAR
AN
DER
NASE.

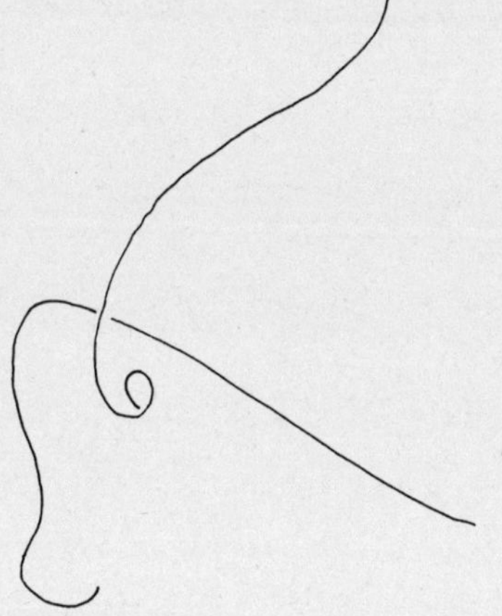

Nose, plus someone else's hair.

VIRUS.

DIE
EIERLEGENDE
WOLL
MILCH
SAU.

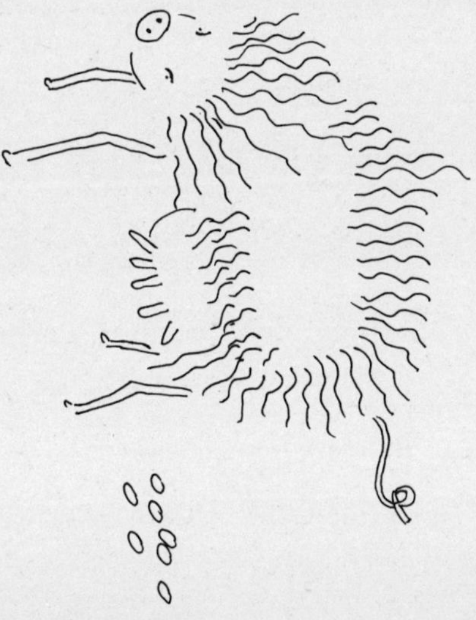

Egg-laying, lactating woolly sow.

Mould cheese. Courageous invention.

DER SCHIMMELKÄSE.
MUTIGE ERFINDUNG.

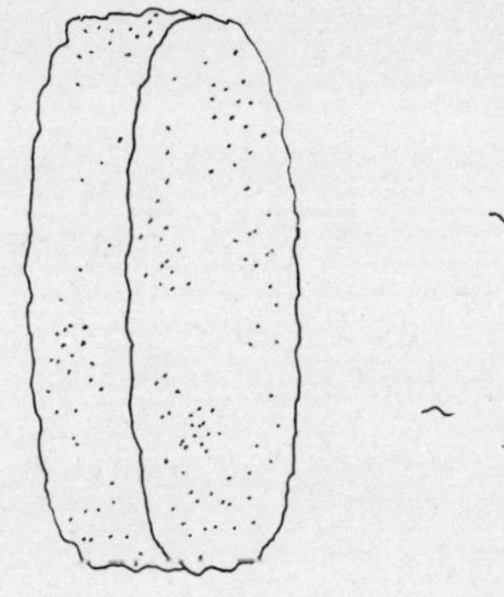

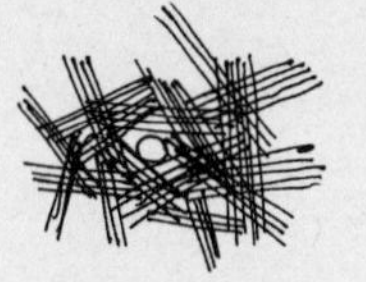

The world of the earthworm.

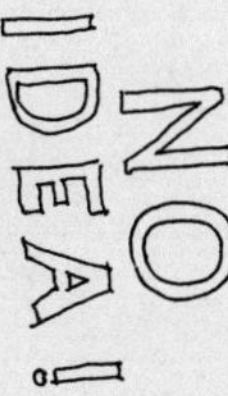
NO
IDEA!

ZAUBERER.

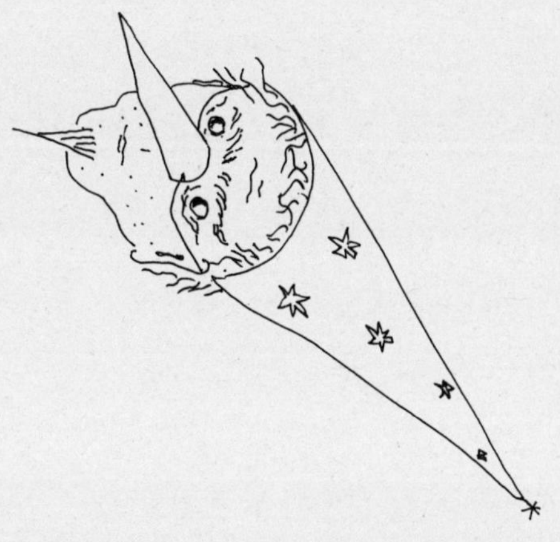

Magician.

The arc of whipped cream on the football pitch.

DER
SAHNEKREIS
AM
FUSSBALLPLATZ

AMEISEN
IM
BALLETT
.

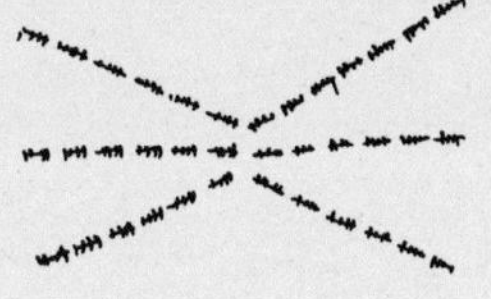

Ants in ballet formation.

How big is a tuna?

WIE
GROSS
IST
EIN
THUNFISCH
?

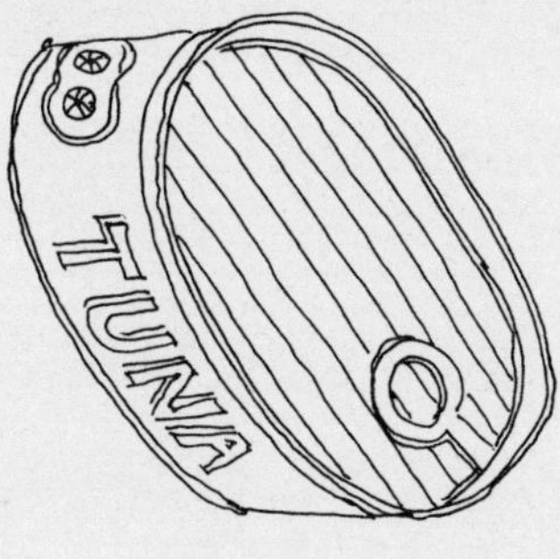

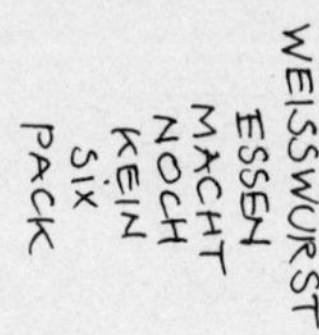

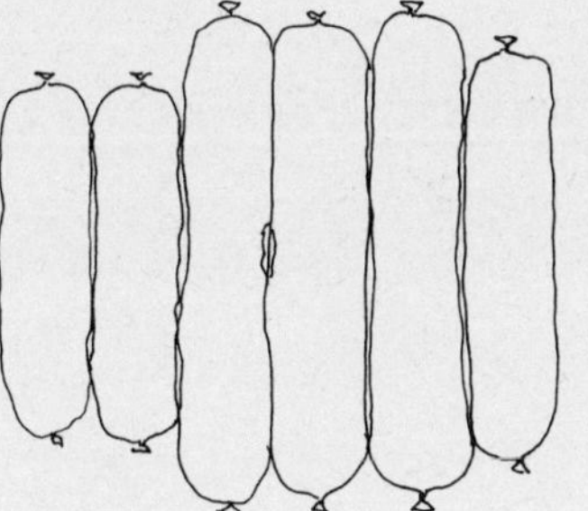

Eating Weißwurst does not make a six-pack.

Ilse does not like rain.

ILSE
MAG
KEINEN
REGEN.

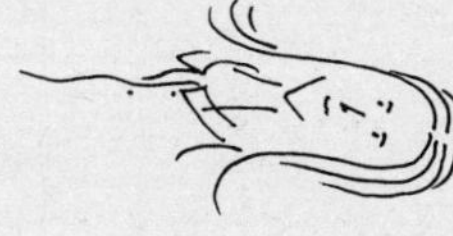

FRANÇOIS
LIEBTE
DEN
REGEN.

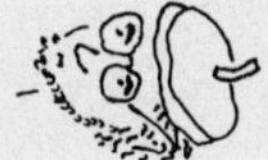

François loved rain.

The judge with the tall judge's hat.

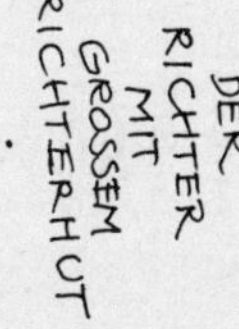

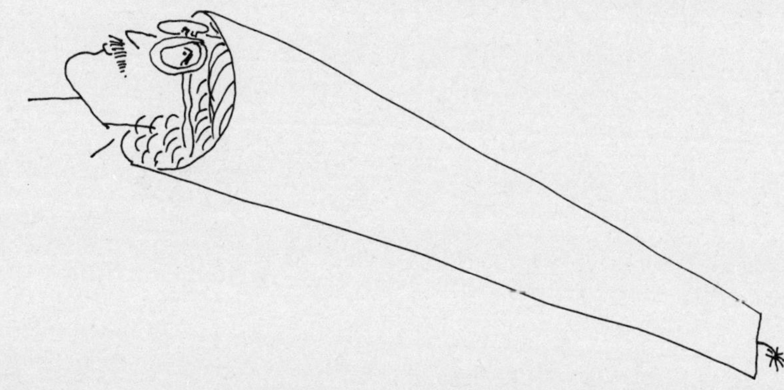

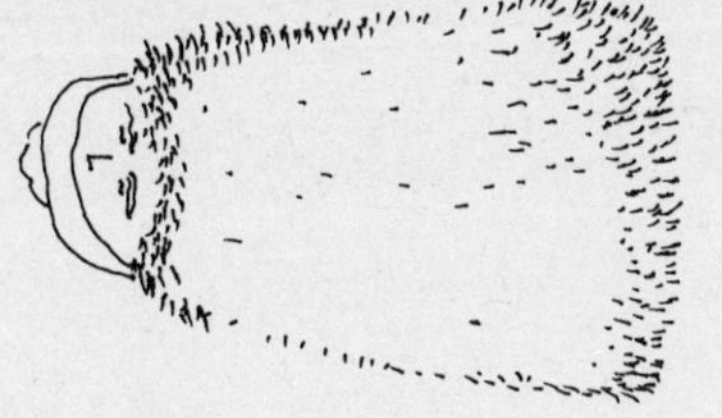

One of the Queen of England's guardsmen.

239 Web.

NETZ

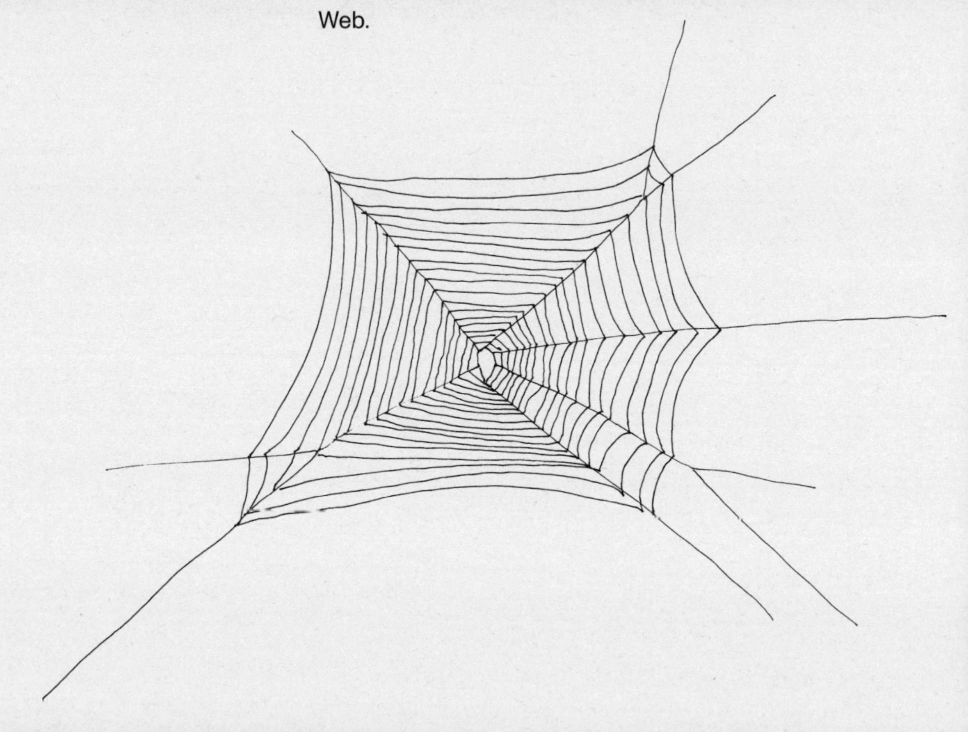

MAKELLOSE
BIRNE.

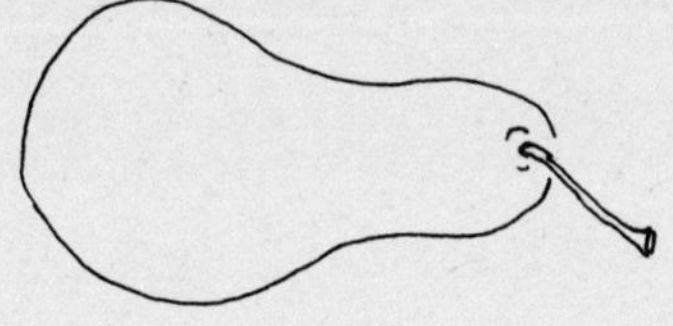

 Flawless pear.

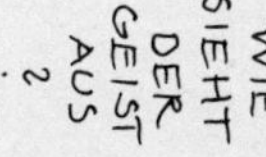
WIE
SIEHT
DER
GEIST
AUS
?

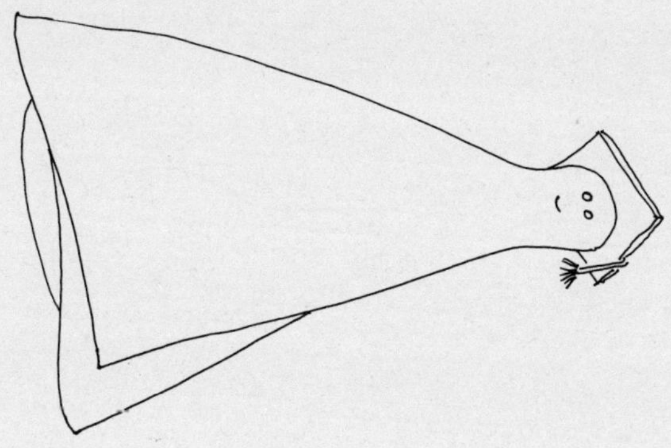

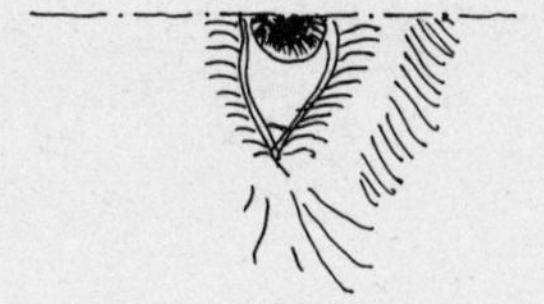

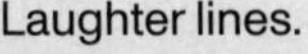

Laughter lines.

He returned from his holiday with a deep tan.

BRAUN
GEBRANNT
KEHRTE
ER
VOM
URLAUB
HEIM.

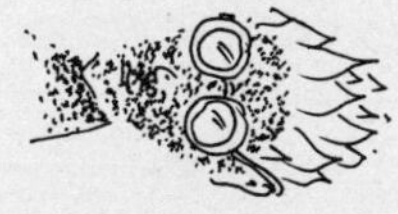

REGEN
IST
FLÜSSIGE
SONNE.

(ERKENNTNIS AUS HAWAII)

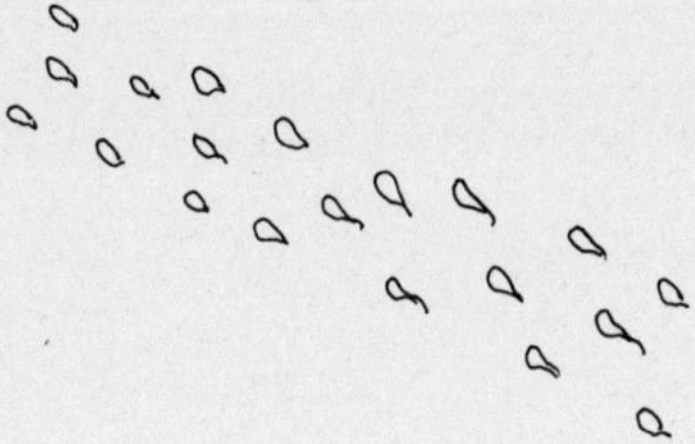

Rain is liquid sunshine. (Insight from Hawaii)

Miami Don Johnson as an ant.

MIAMI
DON
JOHNSON
ALS
AMEISE.

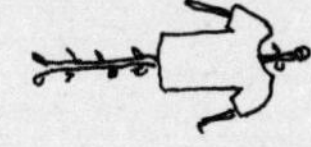

FREI
WIE
EIN
VOGEL
.

Free as a bird.

P with a horn. Nothing's perfect.

P
MIT
HORN
.
NIX
IST
PERFEKT
.

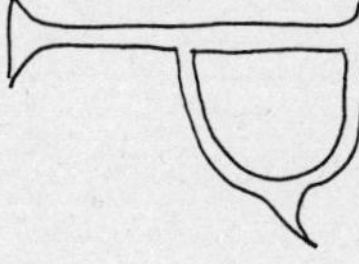

TRIPLE
ERDNUSS
IM
RÖNTGEN.

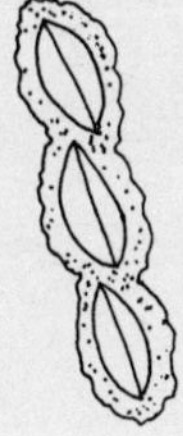

X-ray of a triple peanut.

The pharmacist in his specklessly white lab coat.

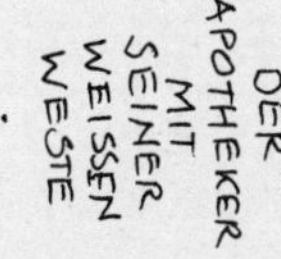

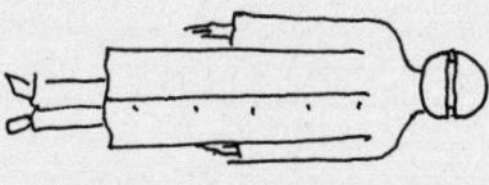

AMEISEN
IM
GLEICHSCHRITT

Ants in lockstep.

Stressed ant.

AMEISE IM STRESS.

AMEISEN
IM
STREIK.

Ants on strike.

Tired as a turkey-stag-horse ...

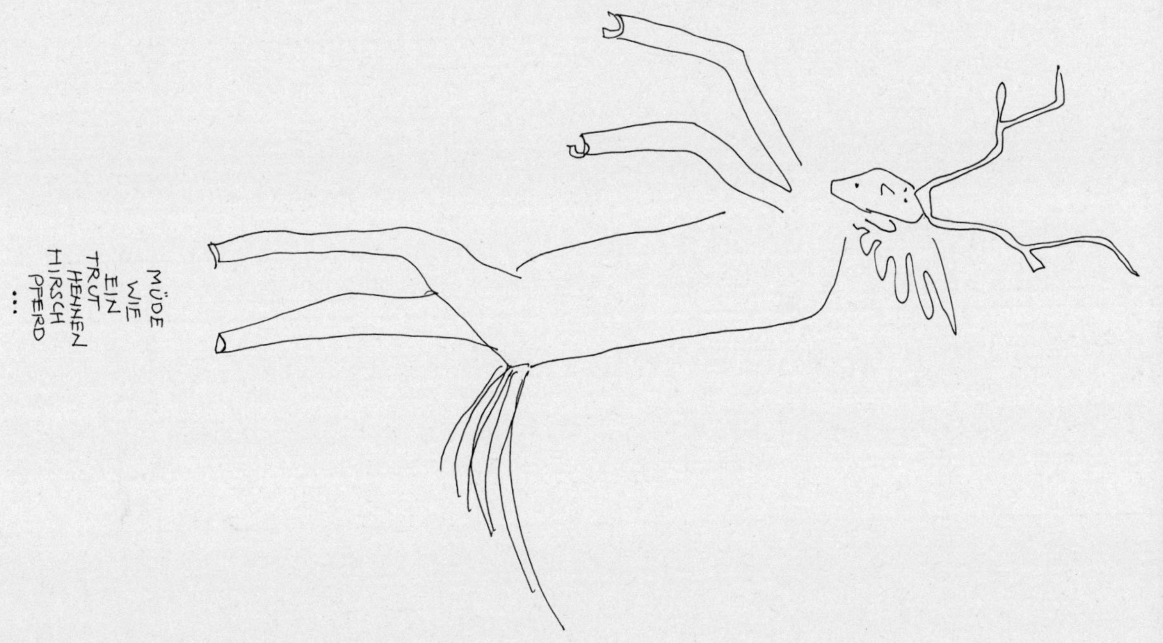

DAS
GLÜCK
IM
SPIEGEL
.

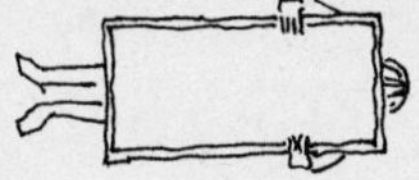

Happiness in a mirror.

Two like-minded ants.

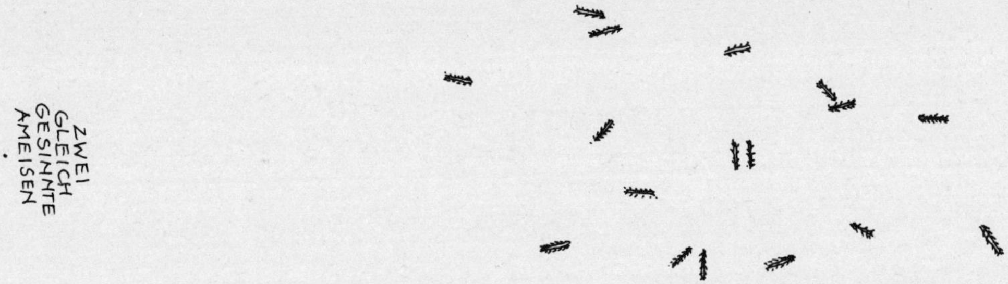

ZWEI GLEICH GESINNTE AMEISEN.

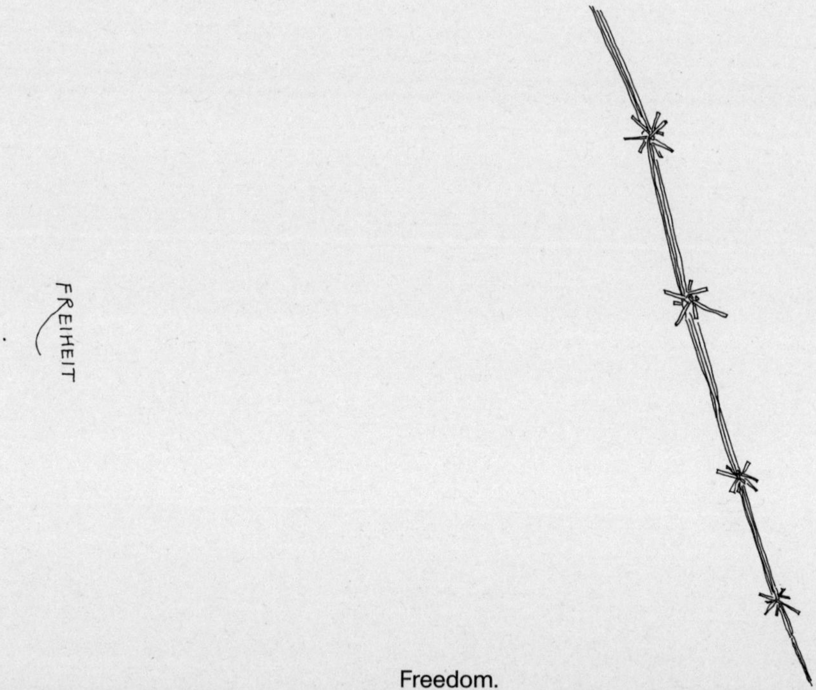

FREIHEIT

Freedom.

Sand brush on the sand.

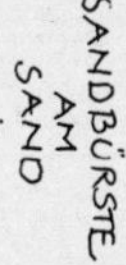

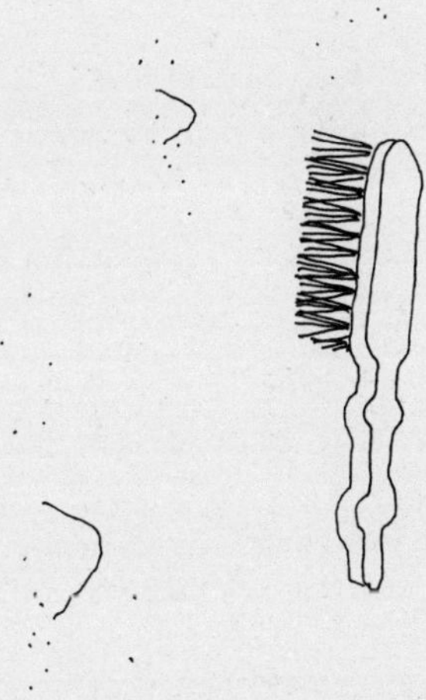

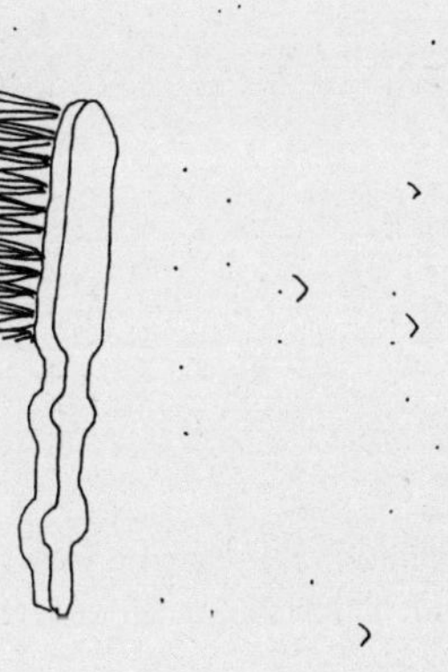

DIE
RITTER
RÜSTUNG
IST
HART.

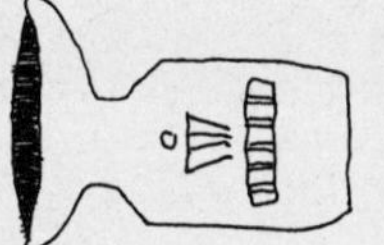

The coat of armour is hard.

Zeus faced with the existential question: farsighted or otherwise?

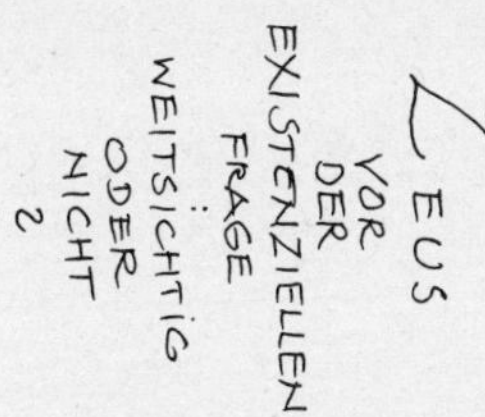

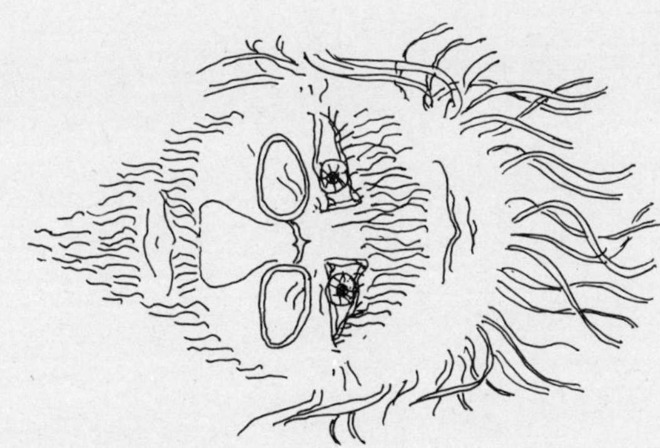

ZEUS IM URLAUB AM MEER.

Zeus on holiday by the sea.

The sea has a memory.

DAS
MEER
HAT
EIN
GEDÄCHTNIS
.

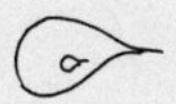

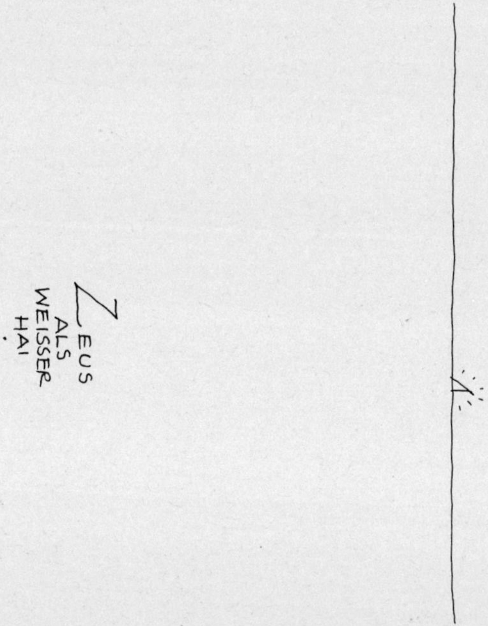

ZEUS
ALS
WEISSER
HAI.

Zeus as a great white shark.

The tear in the jeans was carefully tended.

DER
RISS
IN
DER
JEAN
WURDE
GEHEGT
UND
GEPFLEGT.

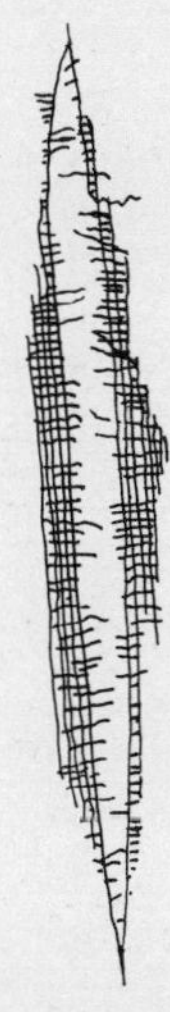

AUSSER
SICH
SELBST

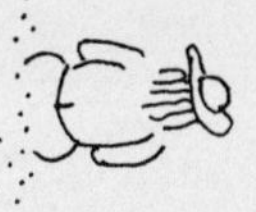

HATTE
DER
TOURIST
NUR
SCHÖNE
SACHEN
UM
SICH.

Apart from himself, the tourist was exclusively surrounded by beautiful things.

Oil was not an idea that olives came up with themselves.

KEINE
DER
OLIVEN
HAT
DAS
ÖL
ERFUNDEN.

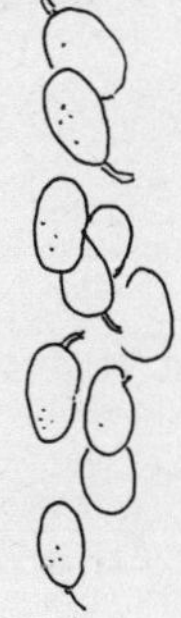

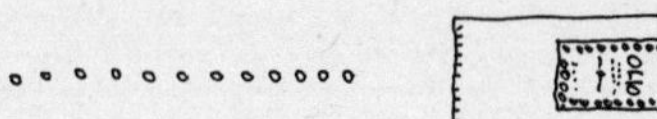

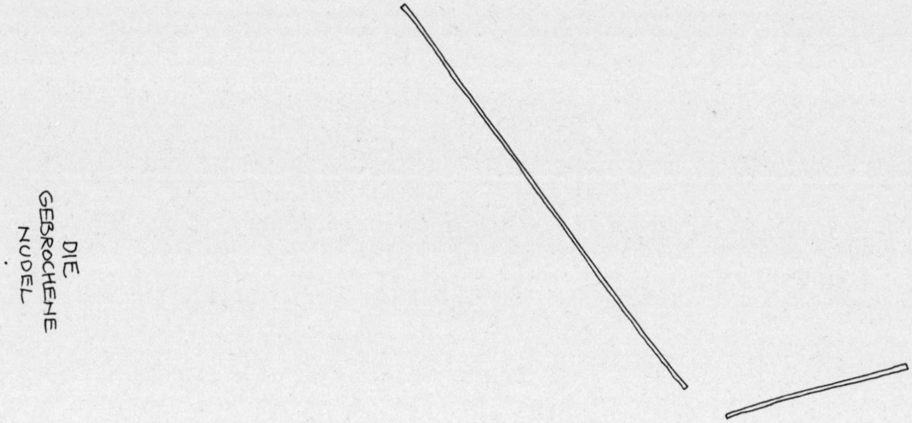

DIE
GEBROCHENE
NUDEL
.

The broken noodle.

Zeus confronted with a red light.

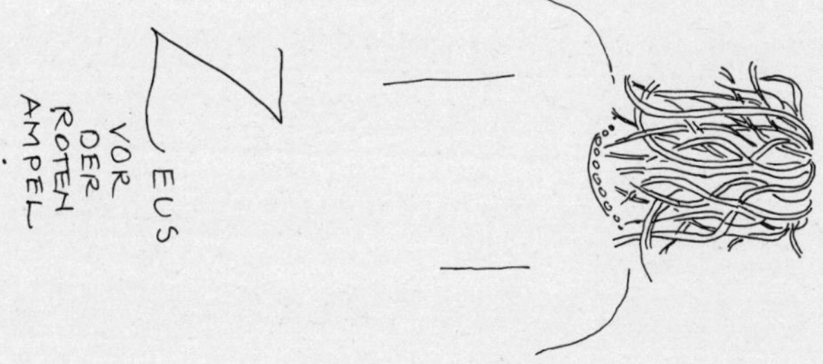

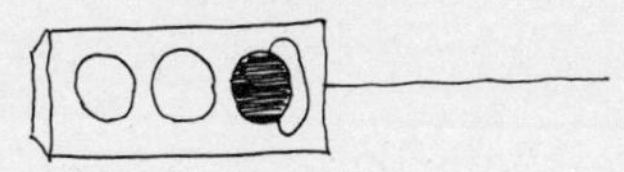

EIN
HEILIGER
ORT.

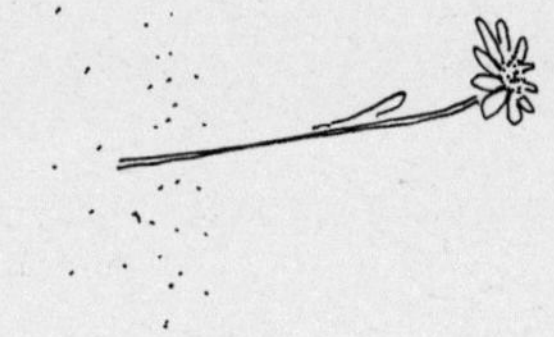

A sacred place.

The Queen always has to sit up straight.

DIE
QUEEN
MUSS
IMMER
GERADE
SITZEN.

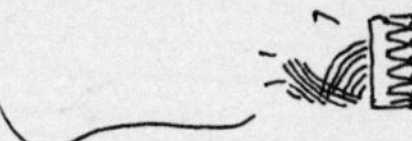

DURCH
DAS
NICHTSTUEN
WURDEN
SIE
KUGELRUND.

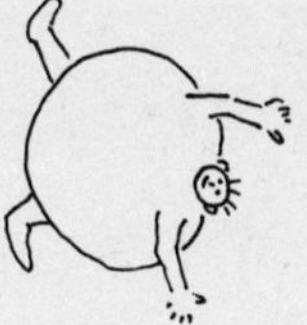

Loafing made them spherical.

To quarrel. A word painting in English.

TO
QUARREL
.
LAUTMALEREI
AUF
ENGLISCH
.

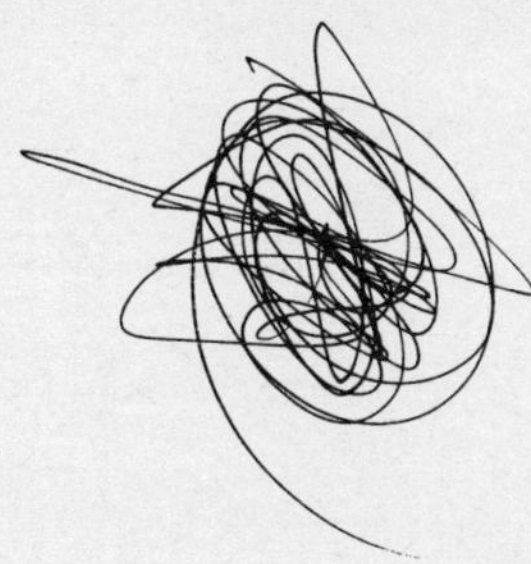

BEGNADETE
KÖRPER.

Finally, everything. Locks cut straight.

ENDLICH
ALLES
.
DER
LOCKEN
GERADE
SCHNITT
.

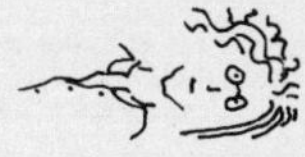

SCHEUES
REH
HINTER
DÜNNEM
BAUM
.

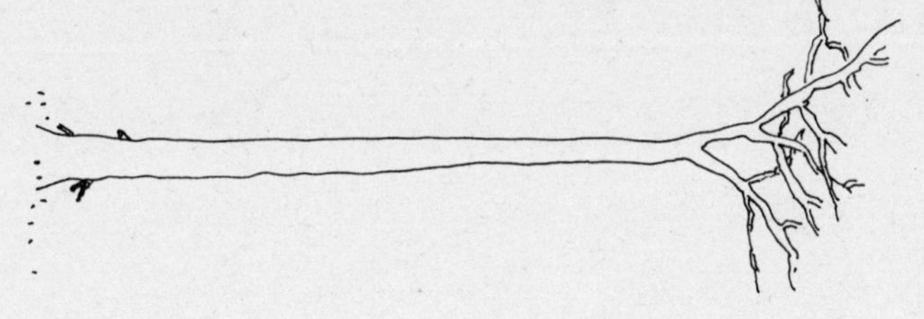

Shy deer behind a thin tree.

Shy stag behind a tree.

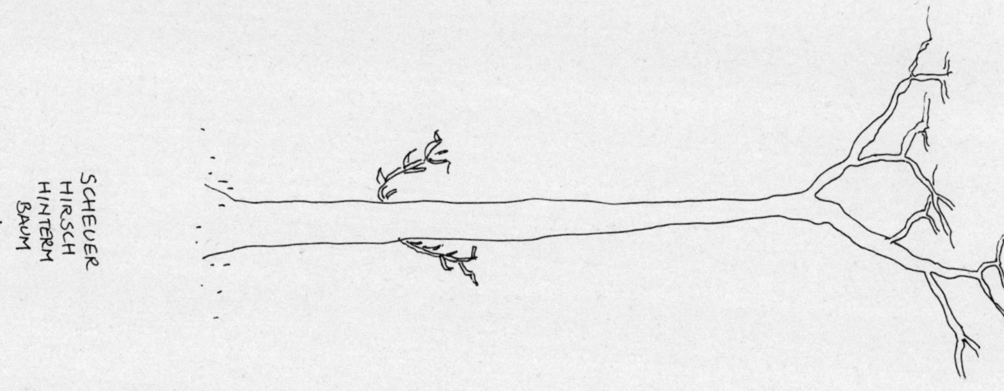

DRAUSSEN
SCHNEE
.

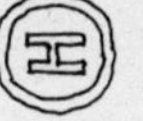

IM
THEATER
HUSTEN
ZUCKERL
.

Outside, snow. In the theatre, cough sweets.

Small eyes. Big glasses.

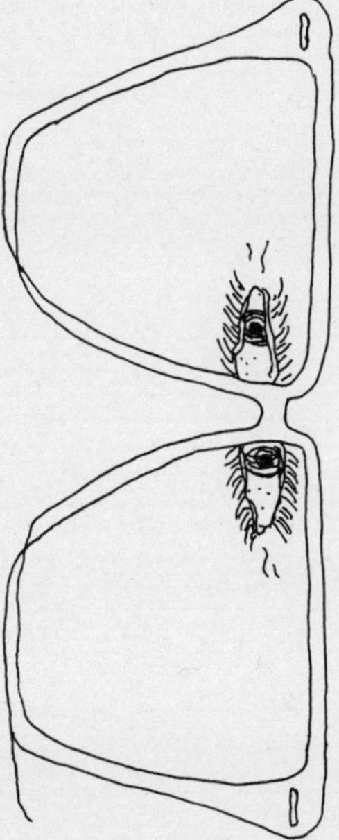

KLEINE AUGEN. GROSSE BRILLE.

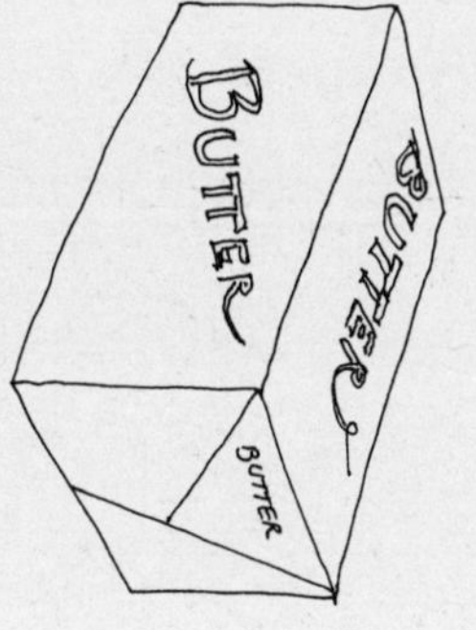

WELCHE
IST
DIE
BUTTERSEITE
.

Which is the buttered side?

Happy kid’s eyes behind a mask of flowers.

GLÜCKLICHE
KINDERAUGEN
HINTER
BLUMEN
MASKE
.

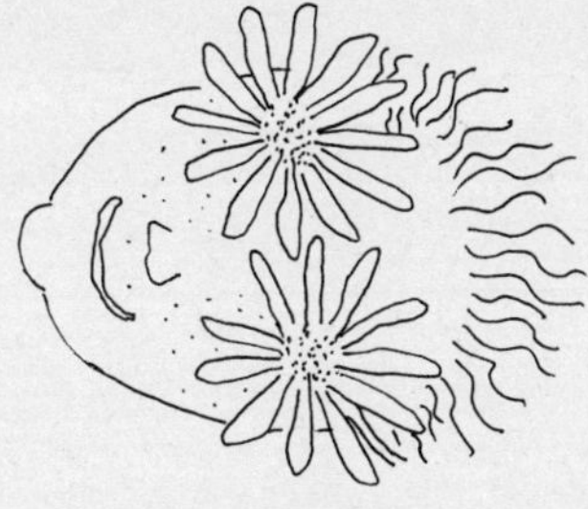

EITEL
WAR
ER
SEHR.

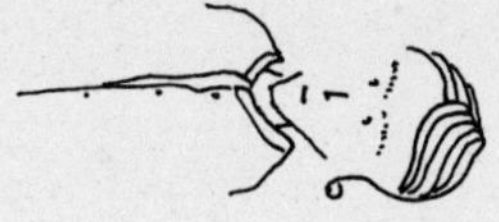

He was very vain.

Telltale noodle stain on the shirt.

TYPISCHER
NUDEL
FLECK
AM
HEMD.

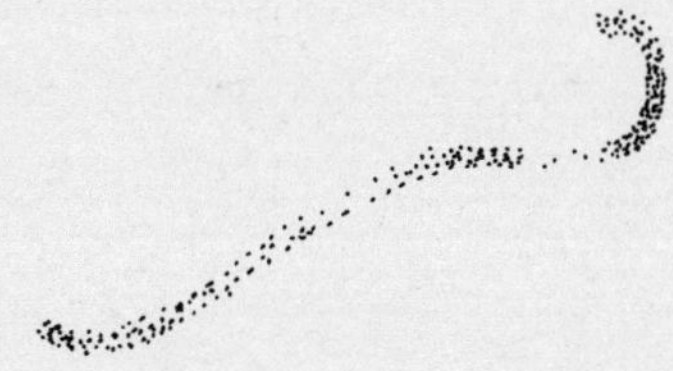

DAS
TANZBEIN.

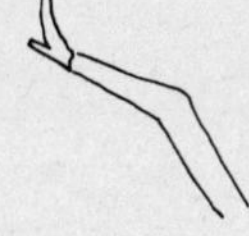

Striking leg.

First chair on the terrace.

ERSTER
STUHL
AUF
DER
TERRASSE

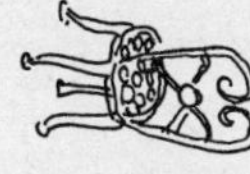

DAS
LEBEN
EINER
MUSCHEL
IST
TOTAL
ANDERS.

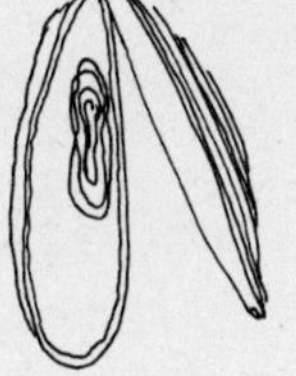

The life of a clam is totally different.

This particular chicken bone may bump you off.

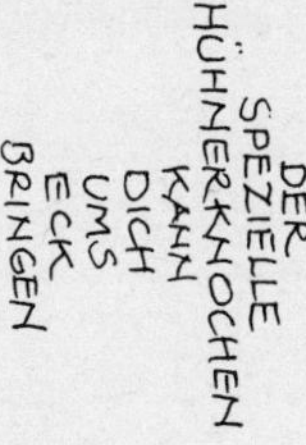

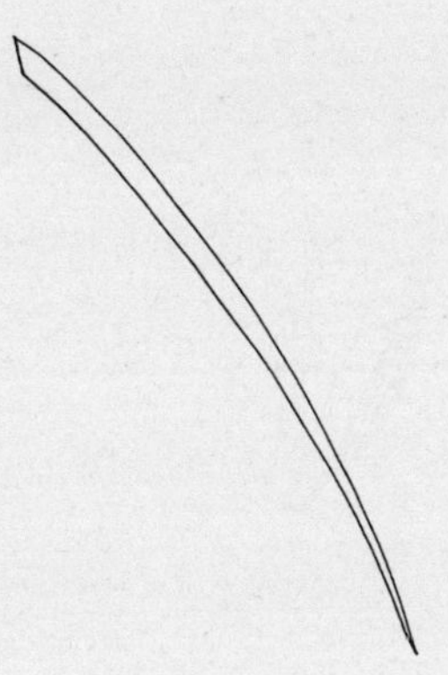

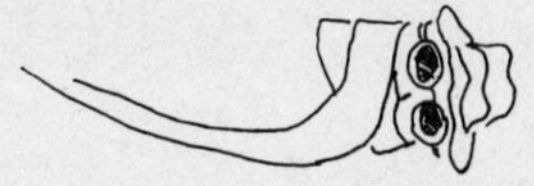

A model, at last.

Inebriated Easter egg.

BETRUNKENES
OSTEREI.

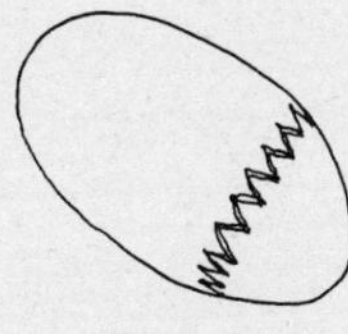

WENN
DER
APFEL
GRÖSSER
ALS
DAS
GESICHT.

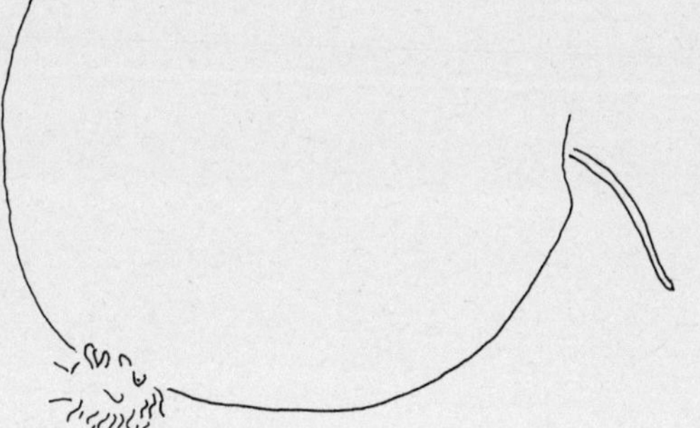

When the apple is bigger than the face.

The stiletto-heeled shoe tried to reach the sky.

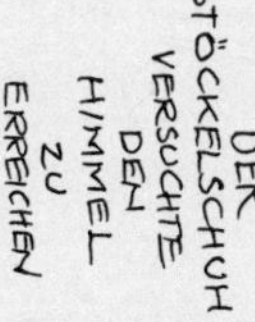

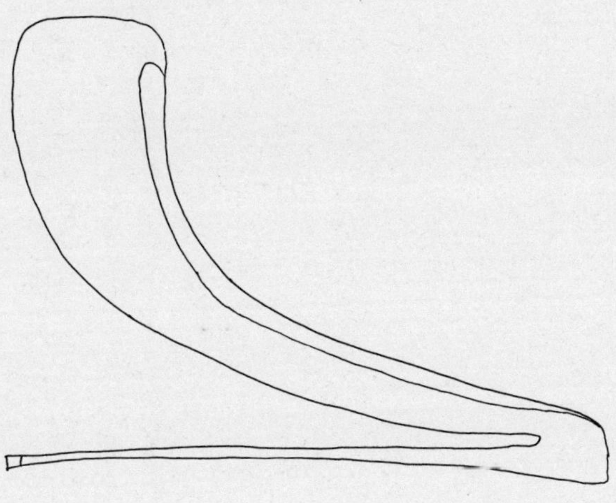

VERGNÜGTES
PFLÄNZCHEN.

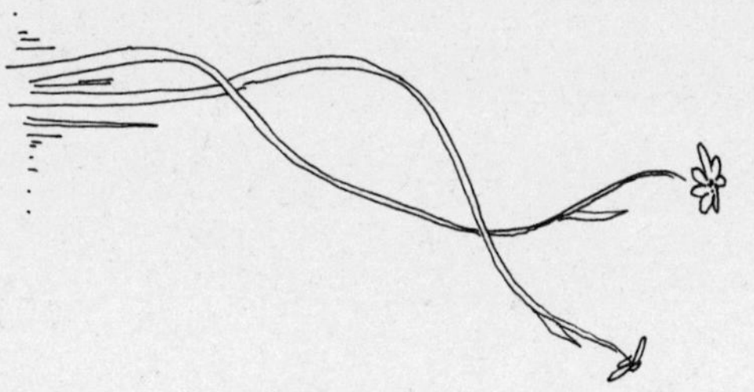

Little plant full of beans.

The ant at its wits' end.

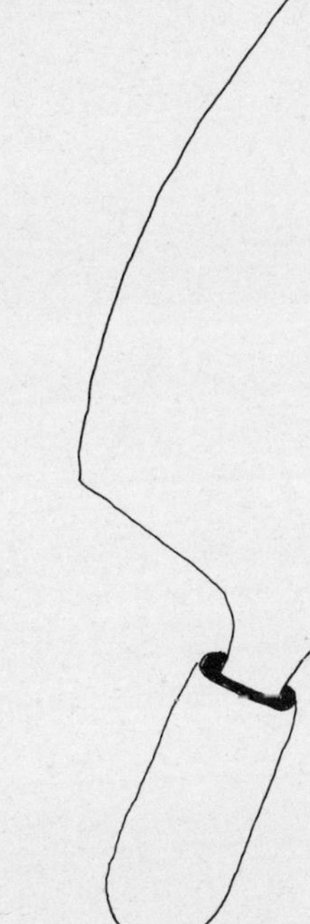

DIE
GRENZE
DER
AMEISE
.

WAS
KANN
AN
EINER
NUSS
SCHON
FALSCH
SEIN
?

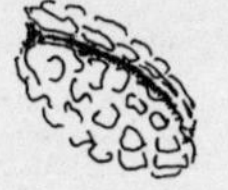

Is there anything that can be wrong about a nut?

The smallest possible tattoo consisted of two dots.

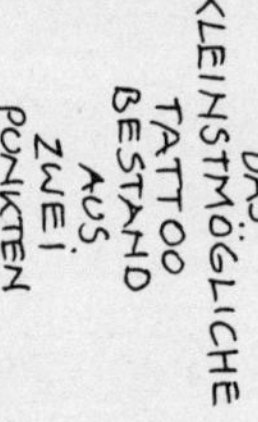

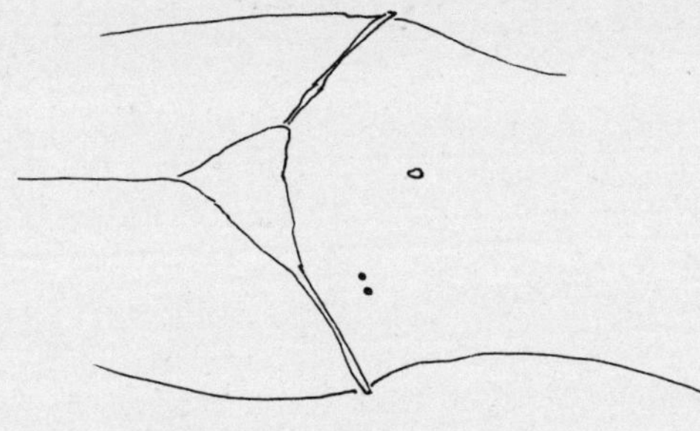

LINKE
SOCKE
BARFUSS.

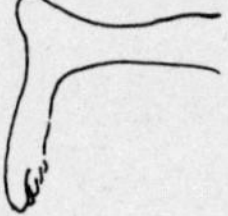

Left sock barefoot.

Zeus hiding behind the sun.

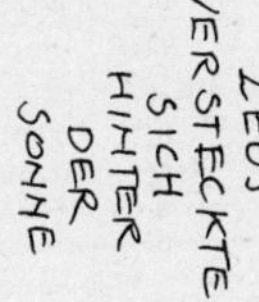

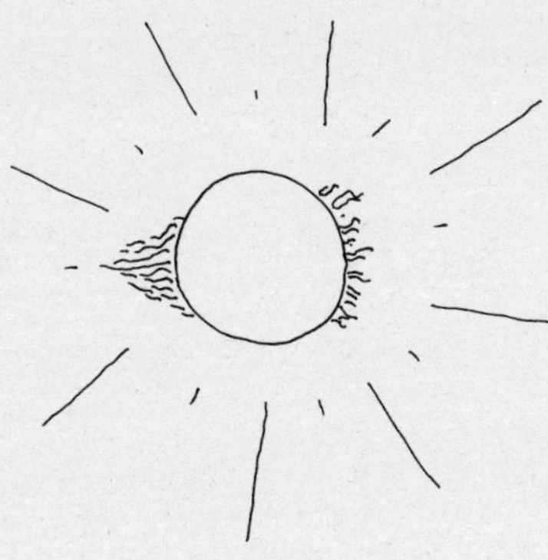

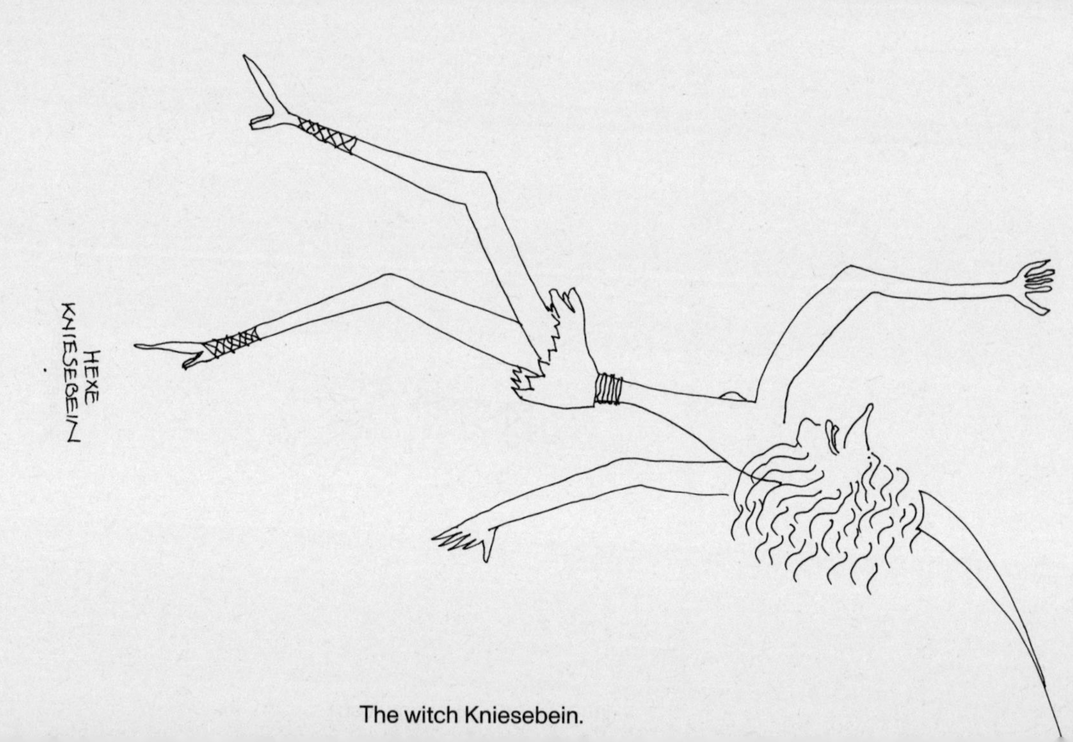

The witch Kniesebein.

The witch Kniesebein (detail).

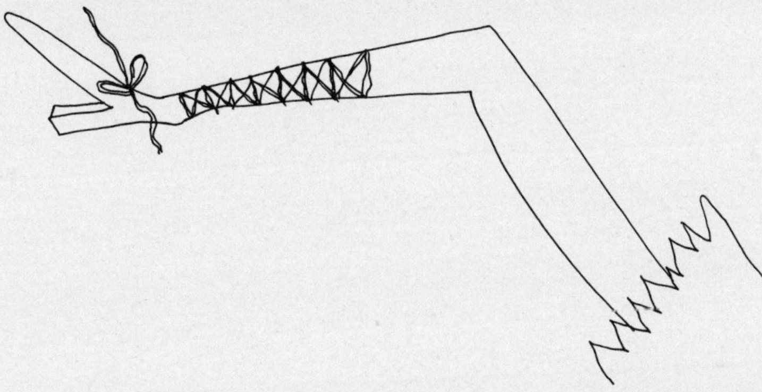

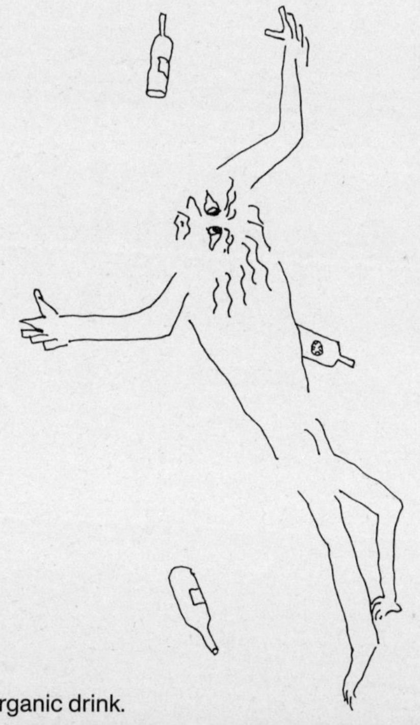

Pissed on strictly organic drink.

When the headband becomes part of a uniform.

WENN
DAS
STIRNBAND
ZUR
UNIFORM
WIRD.

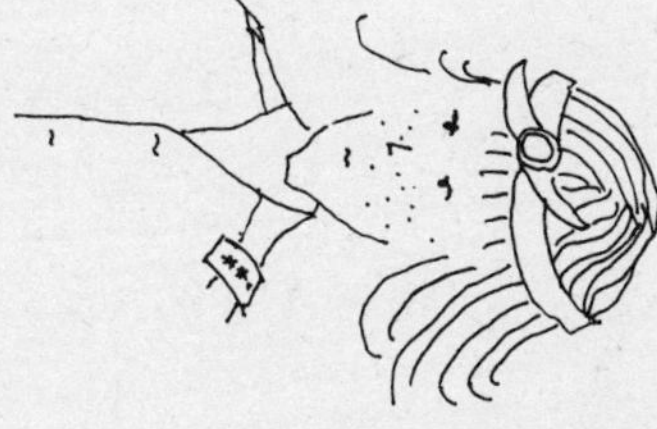

LIEBESBRIEFE
IM
MISTKÜBEL.

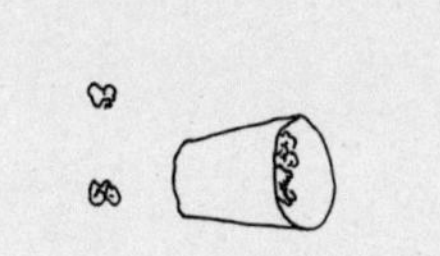

Love letters in a rubbish bin.

Moon and stars in the diary.

MOND
UND
STERNE
IM
TAGEBUCH.

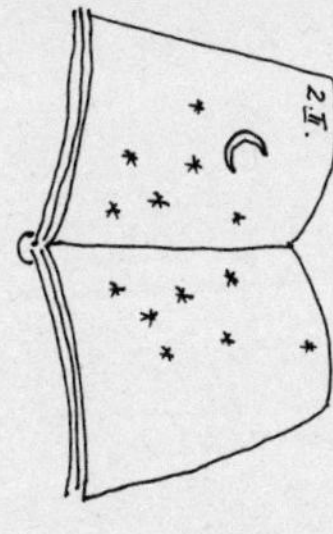

DER
AUTOBUSFAHRER
HATTE
EINE
HERZENBRILLE
AUF
DER
NASE.

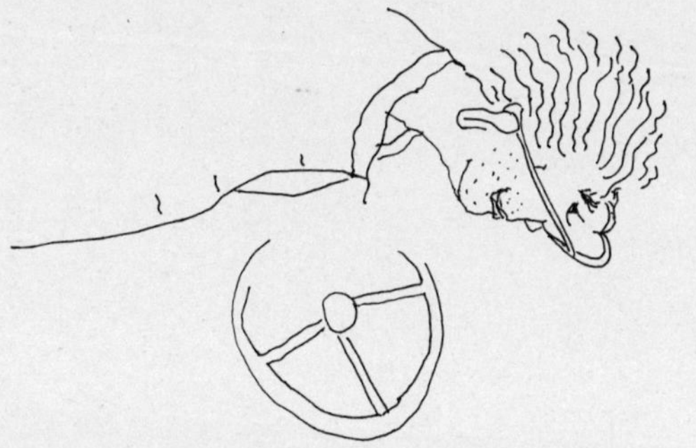

The bus driver sported heart-shaped glasses.

Right speed?

RICHTIGES
TEMPO
?

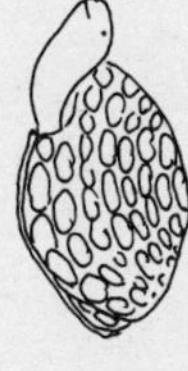

MIT
DER
MAUS
EINEN
GANZEN
TAG
GELÖSCHT
.

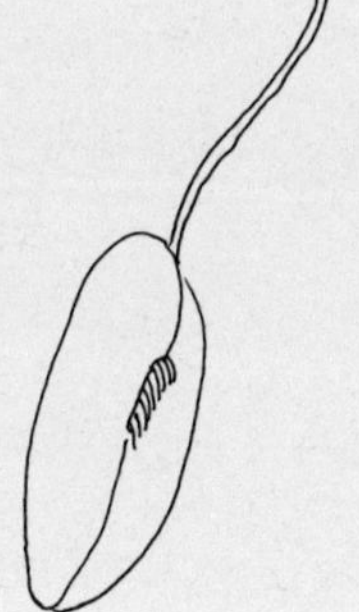

A day's worth of work deleted with one click of the mouse.

So small with a hat.

SO KLEIN MIT HUT.

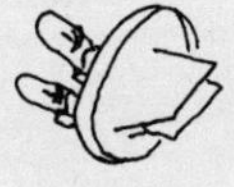

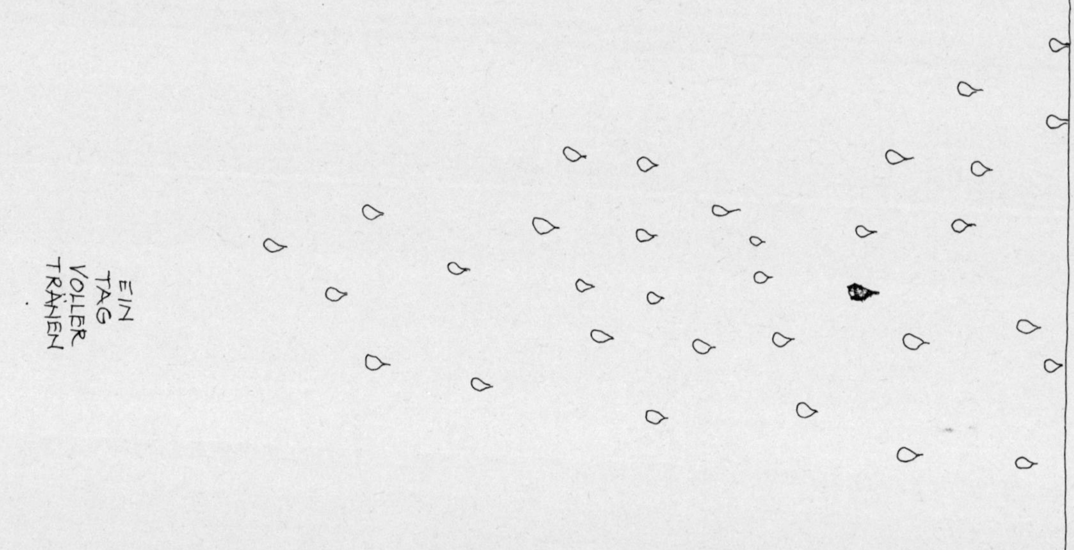

A tearful day.

Soul like a butterfly.

SEELE
WIE
EIN
SCHMETTERLING
.

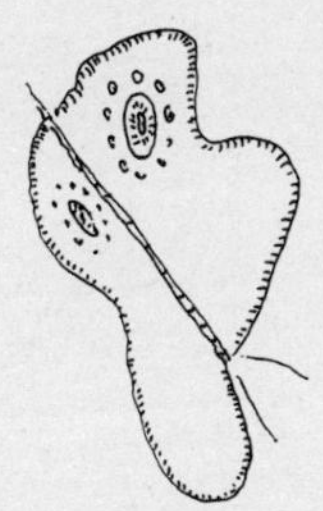

HAT
DIE
OMA
DIE
WÄRMEFLASCHE
ERFUNDEN
?

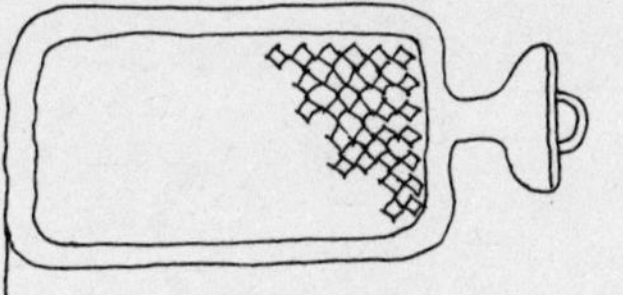

Did granny invent the hot water bottle?

Mask.

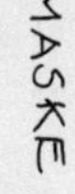

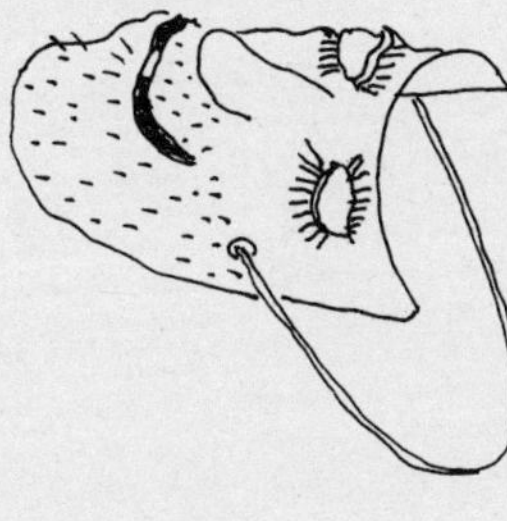

EWIG
DAS
GELD.

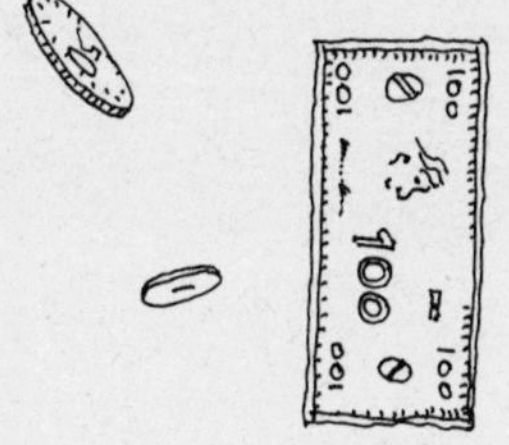

No getting away from money.

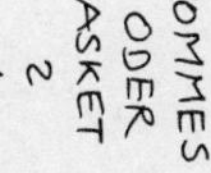
POMMES
ODER
ASKET
?

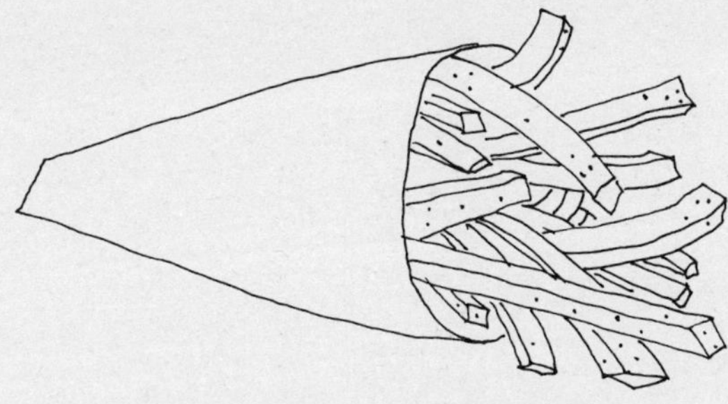

FISCH
IM
GLÜCK
.

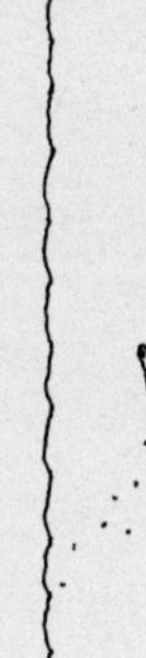

Fish, jubilant.

Do you really want to own a clipping of one of Albert Einstein's toenails?

WILL
MAN
EINEN
ZEHENNAGEL
ALBERT
EINSTEINS
BESITZEN
?

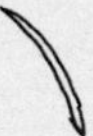

WELTBILD
GOLD

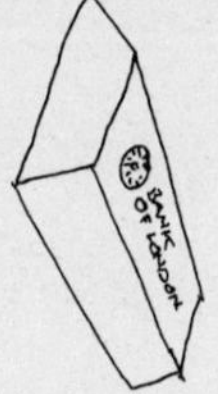

Worldview gold.

He takes football very seriously.

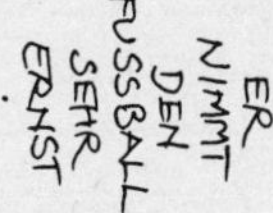

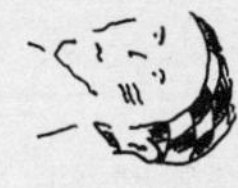

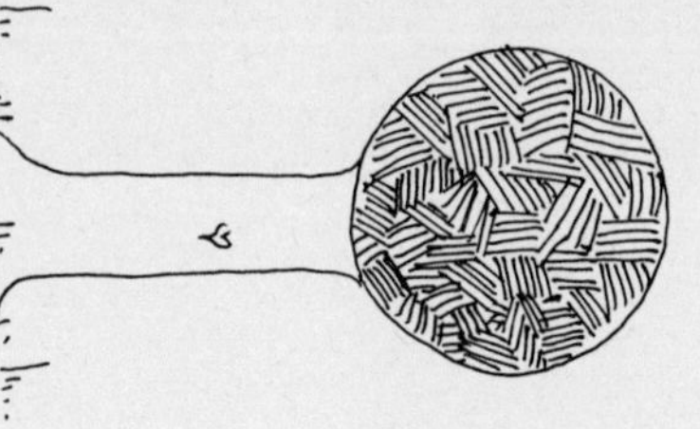

What might the cotton tree look like?

317 Fan without blades.

VENTILATOR
OHNE
FLÜGEL

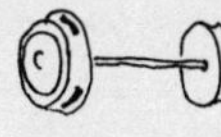

ALLES
AUF
EINE
KARTE.

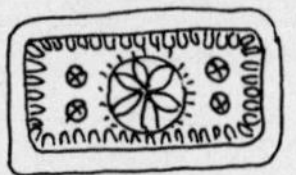

All on one card.

Göttweig	20.08.11	Sandalen	Sandals	019
Wien	22.08.11	Orangenhaut	Orange skin	020
	23.08.11	8000er	Eight-thousanders	021
	24.08.11	Gespenster	Ghosts	022
		Herzen	Hearts	023
	25.08.11	Anfang	Beginning	024
		Tränen	Tears	025
	28.08.11	Bäume	Trees	026
	01.09.11	Wein	Glass	027
		Wunder	Marvel	028
Amsterdam	03.09.11	Ehre	Honour	029
		Sterne	Stars	030
Wien	06.09.11	Glatzen	Bald heads	031
	07.09.11	Unvollendet	Unfinished	032
		Bart	Beard	033
	08.09.11	Fleisch	Meat	034
	09.09.11	Häuser	Houses	035
	10.09.11	Schlafen	Dream	036
Sardinien	15.09.11	Ameisen	Ants	037
		Kakteen	Cacti	038
	17.09.11	Elefanten	Elephants	039
		Meer	Ocean	040
	18.09.11	Schmuck	Jewellery	041
		1000 Jahre	1000 years	042
		1000 Jahre 2	1000 years 2	043

Sardinien	21.09.11	Halten	Saving	044
	22.09.11	Leben	Molto agitato	045
	23.09.11	Seelen	Souls	046
		Faul	Lazy	047
	24.09.11	Regen	Rain	048
		Sonne	Sun	049
Wien	05.10.11	Genug	Plenty	050
		Musik	Music	051
	06.10.11	Jobs	Jobs	052
	13.10.11	Leben	Life	053
		Lotto	Lottery	054
St. Petersburg	16.10.11	Ruhe	Quiet	055
Wien	22.10.11	Sparen	Economise	056
	29.10.11	Schwer	Down	057
		Leicht	Up	058
	30.10.11	Groß	Big	059
		Hei	Hay	060
	01.11.11	Schlafen	Sleeping	061
	20.11.11	Kaffee	Coffee	062
	13.12.11	Gier	Greed	063
	31.12.11	Preis	Price	064
Salzburg	06.01.12	Weihnachtsmann	Father Christmas	065
		Musik	Music	066
Wien	04.02.12	Sehen	Lookout	067
Looshaus Semmering	18.02.12	Detail	Detail	068

Wien	13.05.12	Silikonbrüste	Silicone breasts	069
	14.05.12	Hirn	Brainful	070
	27.05.12	Einfach	Simple	071
	03.06.12	Regen	Rain	072
Kappadokien	14.06.12	Hals	Neck	073
	16.06.12	Welt	World	074
		Lupe	Magnifying	075
Wien	05.07.12	Bilder	Pictures	076
	06.07.12	Verwurzelt	Rooted	077
	07.07.12	Gewicht	Weight	078
	15.07.12	Barthaare	Whiskers	079
Göttweig	23.07.12	Kraft	Power	080
	24.07.12	Clowns	Clowns	081
		Schule	Lesson	082
		Geheimnis	Secret	083
	26.07.12	Schweinehund	Weaker self	084
		Staub	Pollen	085
		Irgendwann	Stage	086
	27.07.12	Hirsche	Deer	087
		Gänsehaut	Goosebumps	088
Triest	29.07.12	Hemden	Shirts	089
	30.07.12	Berührend	Touching	090
	04.08.12	Vergil	Virgil	091
Wien	10.08.12	Nase	Nose	092
	13.08.12	Zart	Tender	093

Wien	13.08.12	Stock	Stick	094
	15.08.12	Wimpern	Blink	095
Venedig	28.08.12	Nudel	Noodle	096
		Pflanzen	Plant	097
Wien	01.09.12	Tomaten	Tomatoes	098
	12.09.12	Rad	Bike	099
	16.09.12	Jung	Young	100
Venedig	23.09.12	Offen	Open	101
Moskau	28.09.12	Bequem	Comfy	102
Wien	18.10.12	Boden	Floor	103
	19.10.12	Tagebuch	Diary	104
	01.11.12	Groß	Tall	105
	13.11.12	Optimiert	Optimised	106
	08.12.12	Viel	Stories	107
		Verkehrt	Wrong direction	108
		Lächeln	Smiling	109
Kuba	22.12.12	Bewölkt	Clouded	110
		Zuviel	Too much	111
	24.12.12	Geräusche	Sound	112
	27.12.12	Schwer	Heavy	113
		Leicht	Light	114
	28.12.12	Scheu	Timid	115
Trinidad	29.12.12	Decke	Blanket	116
	02.01.13	Macht	Power	117
Kuba	06.01.13	Selber	Yourself	118

Kuba	07.01.13	Friede	Peace	119
Heidelberg	11.01.13	Klar	Clear	120
Wien	13.01.13	Parmesan	Parmesan	121
	05.02.13	Ohren	Ears	122
	09.02.13	Lebenslang	For life	123
		Krone	Crown	124
	02.03.13	Sushi	Chopsticks	125
	04.03.13	Haar	Hair	126
		Scham	Shame	127
	20.03.13	Garantie	Guarantee	128
London	09.05.13	Steif	Stiff	129
	10.05.13	Stehen	Feet	130
Wien	15.05.13	Früchte	Fruit	131
	18.05.13	Leben	Life	132
		Absurd	Absurd	133
	24.05.13	Weggeblasen	Blink of an eye	134
Bernstein	30.05.13	Geister	Spirits	135
Neapel	16.06.13	Höhepunkte	High points	136
Wien	22.06.13	Oben	Top	137
	23.06.13	Giacometti	Giacometti	138
	14.08.13	Grenze	Border	139
	24.08.13	Nichts	Nothing	140
	28.08.13	Streicheln	Stroke	141
	31.08.13	Vielleicht	Perhaps	142
	01.09.13	Fehler	Typo	143

Wien	14.09.13	Er	He	144
	19.09.13	Roboter	Robots	145
	29.09.13	Ende	End	146
München	04.10.13	Vogelmeer	Sea of birds	147
Wien	26.10.13	Erfinder	Inventor	148
	27.10.13	Selten	Unusual	149
	01.11.13	Winterschlaf	Hibernation mode	150
	07.11.13	Lernen	Learning	151
	09.11.13	Trauer	Mourning	152
	17.11.13	Ausgebrochen	Run	153
	25.12.13	Pflänzchen	Plants	154
		Ozean	Ocean	155
	31.12.13	Baum	Tree	156
		Träne	Tear	157
	01.01.14	Elefant	Elephant	158
	03.01.14	James	James	159
	05.01.14	Streik	Strike	160
	24.01.14	Geister	Spirits	161
	06.02.14	Schlafen	Sleep	162
	07.02.14	Supermarkt	Supermarket	163
	09.02.14	Schalk	Twinkle	164
	11.02.14	Verkürzen	Shortened	165
	22.02.14	Beste	Bee's knees	166
Lanzarote	09.03.14	Essen	Food	167
		Fliegen	Flight	168

Wien	27.09.14	Musik	Music	194
	28.09.14	Baum	Tree	195
	19.10.14	Mond	Moon	196
	22.10.14	Sohn	Son	197
Miami	30.11.14	Minirock	Miniskirt	198
Wien	13.01.15	Ordnung	Order	199
Prag	07.03.15	Erfindung	Invention	200
Ibiza	11.04.15	Sand	Sand	201
	12.04.15	Ganz	Entire	202
	08.05.15	Gummibären	Gummy Bears	203
Wien	27.06.15	Zeit	Time	204
St. Gilgen	08.08.15	Schatz	Treasure	205
Dortmund	14.08.15	Blöd	Stupid	206
		Werk	Work	207
St. Wolfgang	19.08.15	Brauchen	Need	208
	21.08.15	Korn	Corn	209
	04.09.15	Weggeschaut	Looking away	210
		Schaf	Sheep	211
Zürich	09.09.15	Neu	New	212
Wien	13.09.15	Diamant	Diamond	213
München	22.09.15	Persönlich	Intimate	214
Wien	25.09.15	Krieger	Warriors	215
	15.10.15	Waage	Scales	216
	18.11.15	Würfel	Cast	217
	22.11.15	Klein	Small	218

Beruwela	22.12.15	Ozean	Ocean	219
	23.12.15	Kompott	Compote	220
	25.12.15	Eigen	Own	221
	27.12.15	Wurzel	Root	222
	29.12.15	FBI	FBI	223
Wien	21.02.16	Nase	Nose	224
	11.03.16	Virus	Virus	225
	20.03.16	Sau	Sow	226
Split	22.04.16	Erfindung	Invention	227
Wien	23.04.16	Welt	World	228
Barcelona	30.04.16	No	No	229
Kitzbühel	28.05.16	Zauberer	Magician	230
Wien	12.06.16	Fussballplatz	Football pitch	231
		Ballett	Ballet	232
		Thunfisch	Tuna	233
	17.06.16	Weißwurst	Weißwurst	234
	20.06.16	Regen	Rain	235
	21.06.16	Regen	Rain	236
St. Wolfgang	15.07.16	Richter	Judge	237
		Königin	Queen	238
		Netz	Web	239
Wien	21.07.16	Makellos	Flawless	240
St. Wolfgang	10.08.16	Geist	Mind	241
	12.08.16	Falten	Lines	242
		Urlaub	Holiday	243

St. Wolfgang	13.08.16	Sonne	Sunshine	244
Wien	27.08.16	Ameise	Ant	245
	29.08.16	Frei	Free	246
	31.08.16	Perfekt	Perfect	247
	03.09.16	Erdnuss	Peanut	248
	07.09.16	Weiß	White	249
Brüssel	15.09.16	Gleichschritt	Lockstep	250
Steinbach	16.09.16	Stress	Stressed	251
		Streik	Strike	252
Sardinien	20.09.16	Müde	Tired	253
	21.09.16	Spiegel	Mirror	254
	23.09.16	Gleich	Like	255
	25.09.16	Freiheit	Freedom	256
	26.09.16	Sand	Sand	257
	27.09.16	Ritter	Armour	258
	28.09.16	Zeus	Zeus	259
		Zeus	Zeus	260
		Gedächtnis	Memory	261
	29.09.16	Hai	Shark	262
	30.09.16	Riss	Tear	263
Cagliari	02.10.16	Außer	Apart	264
Wien	03.10.16	Öl	Oil	265
	10.10.16	Nudel	Noodle	266
	14.10.16	Rot	Red	267
	23.10.16	Ein	A	268

Wien	02.09.17	Linke	Left	294
Santorin	10.09.17	Sonne	Sun	295
Wien	30.10.17	Hexe	Witch	296
		Kniesebein	Kniesebein	297
Venedig	17.11.17	Bio	Organic	298
		Uniform	Uniform	299
Wien	27.01.18	Liebesbriefe	Love letters	300
	02.02.18	Tagebuch	Diary	301
	03.02.18	Herzensbrille	Heart-shaped glasses	302
	09.02.18	Richtig	Right	303
	10.03.18	Gelöscht	Deleted	304
	11.03.18	Hut	Hat	305
Heidelberg	24.03.18	Tränen	Tearful	306
Wien	29.04.18	Seele	Soul	307
	01.05.18	Oma	Granny	308
Wachau	15.05.18	Maske	Mask	309
Split	31.05.18	Geld	Money	310
		Asket	Nada	311
	02.06.18	Glück	Jubilant	312
Wien	13.06.18	Einstein	Einstein	313
	17.06.18	Gold	Gold	314
Marseille	06.07.18	Ernst	Seriously	315
	07.07.18	Baumwolle	Cotton	316
Arles	09.07.18	Ohne	Without	317
Sète	14.07.18	Alles	All	318

Christian Heiss, geb. 1967 in Wien, widmete sich in jungen Jahren intensiv dem Geigenspiel. Die spätere Beschäftigung mit dem Geigenbau beeinflusste seinen Zugang zur Architektur wesentlich. Das Mystische, den Klang des Instrumentes anhand seiner Form und Schönheit zu ahnen und bereits innerlich zu hören, entspricht für Christian Heiss der Kunst des Architekten, einen Raum und dessen Qualitäten im Vorfeld zu erspüren.

Die familiäre Prägung – sein Vater war ebenfalls Architekt und Städteplaner – legte einen weiteren Grundstein für die gestalterischen Werte und das Verständnis von Stadt

Christian Heiss, born in Vienna in 1967, was a keen violinist in his teens. This led him on to violin making, an experience that was seminal for his approach to architecture. The almost mystical aspect of intuiting the sound of an instrument from its shape and beauty and, as it were, of listening to it with an inner ear, is tantamount for Christian Heiss to the architect's skill of anticipating the feel of a space before it is actually built.

His family background – his father was also an architect and town planner – has contributed significantly to Christian Heiss's values as a designer and to his understanding of the city as a living

bei Christian Heiss: wesentliche Eckpfeiler in seinem Berufsalltag.

Die weitere Auseinandersetzung mit der Faszination Raum erfolgt über das Zeichnen – für Heiss unerlässliche Wahrnehmungsschulung jedes Planers. Im Entwurfsprozess ist die Skizze Sprache der Idee und deren essenzieller Ausdruck.

Die Laufbahn als selbstständiger Architekt begann 1997 zu Hause am Küchentisch. Kurz darauf erfolgten der Wechsel in die Schleifmühlgasse im Herzen Wiens und der kontinuierliche Aufbau des Atelier Heiss.

organism. These are the pillars his professional life rests on.

Heiss further investigates the fascinating field of space in his sketches and drawings, which in his view is indispensable for the training of an architect's perceptual skills. In the design process, the draft is the medium through which an idea articulates itself and achieves essential expression.

Christian Heiss's career as an independent architect first took off in 1997 on the kitchen table at home. This was followed shortly afterwards by the establishment of an architectural practice in Schleifmühlgasse

Im Laufe der Zeit formten sich die Schwerpunkte. Heute arbeiten 25 Angestellte und drei Partner unter seiner Führung an zahlreichen Projekten in den Bereichen Hotel, Wohnen und Büro. Dabei reicht die Bandbreite vom städtebaulichen Konzept bis zur Detailplanung und vom einfachen Wohnbau bis zum 5-Sterne-Hotel. Über 500 verwirklichte Projekte erlauben es Christian Heiss, aus einem reichen Erfahrungsschatz zu schöpfen.

2014 erhielt das Atelier Heiss den Staatspreis für Architektur.

Christian Heiss: „Das Schönste schließlich ist das fertiggestellte

in the heart of Vienna. In the meantime, the practice has grown by leaps and bounds.

Over time, different foci emerged. Today, the practice has a staff of twenty-five and three partners. Projects developed under Heiss's guidance include hotels, residential buildings, and offices, ranging in size from town planning concepts to the minute details, from family houses to five-star hotels. Christian Heiss can draw on the experience of more than 500 realised projects.

In 2014, Atelier Heiss was awarded Austria's State Prize for Architecture.